W9-BTO-326

Cook Your Way Through The S.A.T.

ISBN: 1461194490
ISBN-13: 978-1461194491
LCCN: 2011914520

Charis Freiman-Mendel

Jennie Ann Freiman

Cook Your Way Through The S.A.T.

Recipes Worth A Thousand Words

Illustrations
Alex Larder

To the students who endure the trials and tribulations
of standardized testing:

Good luck and bon appétit!

Acknowledgements

Many thanks to my primary tasters: Mom, Dad, Ross, Ruby, Diego and Jorge. Mom, thank you for being my biggest supporter, teacher, and editor. Dad, thank you for inspiring me to find my passion and run with it. Thanks to Ross, my illustrious brother, for obsessively watching the Food Channel with me and challenging me to "Iron Chef" competitions throughout the years. Thanks to Ruby for helping me become proficient in Creole and being an honest critic. Thanks to my Labradoodles, Diego and Jorge, who were unwavering in their desire to be first in line to taste my creations.

Much appreciation to the recipe contributors, advice givers and my friends.

Special thanks to Alex Larder (http://alexandralarder.daportfolio.com) for her beautiful illustrations and exceptional patience.

How To Use This Book

"Cook Your Way Through The S.A.T." consists of a collection of 99 recipes, 100 fun-fact blurbs and 1000 vocabulary words that frequently appear on the SAT and other standardized tests, including the ACT, PSAT, SSAT, ISEE, COOP, GRE and TOEFL.

Think of a recipe, blurb and word list as a *lesson*. We suggest the reader first skim the recipe and blurb to become familiar with the vocabulary. Assembling the recipe ingredients and cooking the dish provide context for the vocabulary and sensory association with the words. After creating the meal, reread the blurb and take the match test offered at the end of each lesson.

Check your results in the "Index Of Vocabulary By Recipe," the answer key provided at the end of the book.

You can also visit www.SATgourmet.com for an alphabetical list of the 1000 vocabulary words and their definitions.

Have fun!

Charis and Jennie

*RAW EGG WARNING: Use caution in handling and consuming raw and lightly cooked eggs due to the risk of food-borne illness. To reduce this risk, use only AA eggs with unbroken shells and avoid contact between the shell and the egg yolk/egg white.

First Course

Fennel And Pear Salad
Chop Chop Salad
Greek Salad
Watermelon, Feta And Tomato Salad
Lima Bean And Cilantro Salad
Black Bean And Corn Salad
Wedge Salad
Fig And Olive Tapenade On Baked Baguette
Smoked Salmon, Cucumber And Cream Cheese On Baguette
Pea And Prosciutto Soup
Potage Parmentier (Potato Leek Soup)
Corn Chowder
Chicken And Dumpling Soup
Gazpacho
Brussels Sprouts And Mushroom Tart
Pear And Gorgonzola Tart
Sylvia's Steamed Cabbage With Caraway And Ground "Meat"
Nancy's Hummus With Pita Chips
Onion Casserole
Latkes (Potato Pancakes)
Steamed Bok Choy With Collard Greens
Fried Green Tomatoes
Roasted Red Peppers
Spicy Stewed Potatoes
Glazed Carrots
Asparagus With Hollandaise Sauce
Brown Rice With Almonds And Raisins
Fried Plantains
Roasted Butternut Squash With Dried Cranberries
Rosemary and Thyme Scalloped Potatoes
Pork Buns
Vegetable Kabobs
Scallops Gratin

Fennel And Pear Salad
Serves 3

Salad:
2 Bosc pears
1 medium fennel head

Dressing:
1 lemon, juiced
¼ cup extra virgin olive oil
Salt and freshly ground black pepper to taste

Thinly slice the pears and fennel,
and place them in a large bowl.

In a separate bowl, whisk together the
lemon juice, oil, and a pinch of salt and pepper.

Drizzle the dressing over the salad.

Serve.

The MYTHOLOGIC Prometheus is said to have UTILIZED the fennel stalk to LOOT fire from the gods and DISPENSE it to mortals. On a more MUNDANE note, fennel is a perennial herb whose BULBOUS base is used as a vegetable in cooking. Its licorice taste is AKIN to anise, ALBEIT not as strong. It is also an INGREDIENT in absinthe, a highly alcoholic drink which critics REVILE for its addictive quality.

———

MYTHOLOGIC	worldly
UTILIZE	plunder
LOOT	similar
DISPENSE	although
MUNDANE	component
BULBOUS	abuse
AKIN	legendary
ALBEIT	provide
INGREDIENT	round
REVILE	use

Chop Chop Salad
Serves 4

Salad:
2 zucchini
1 ear of corn
½ cucumber
1 avocado
25 grape tomatoes
1 handful of Bibb lettuce or arugula
Salt and freshly ground pepper to taste

Dressing:
½ lemon, juiced
2 tbsp extra virgin olive oil
Salt and freshly ground pepper to taste

Preheat a grill pan to a medium heat and drizzle with olive oil. Cut the zucchini in half lengthwise and place on the grill with 1 ear of corn. Allow the zucchini to cook on each side for 7 minutes or until golden. Turn the corn every 5 minutes and cook for 10 minutes or until the corn becomes bright yellow in color. Remove from the pan and turn off the heat. Allow the corn and zucchini to cool before chopping.

Halve the grape tomatoes, and cut the cucumber and zucchini into bite size pieces. Cut the avocado in half, remove the pit, score and scoop out the meat with a spoon. Hold the corn upright and slide a knife down it gently to remove the kernels.

Place all of the vegetables and lettuce (or arugula) into a bowl and toss gently.

Whisk together all of the ingredients for the dressing, pour over the salad and toss.

Serve immediately.

"Chop chop" has an interesting ETYMOLOGY: it's thought to be rooted in the Chinese "kwai kwai," which translates to "hurry up, ACCELERATE, get a move on, make HASTE." "Chop" means to "HEW" or "hack," but when doubled and CONJOINED as "chop chop," its CONNOTATION changes, becoming a PITHY command designed to GALVANIZE even the laziest person to action. Do not use this IMPIOUS term to ADMONISH your college counselor if he or she is running late!

ETYMOLOGY	concise
ACCELERATE	cut
HASTE	warn
HEW	disrespectful
CONJOIN	animate
CONNOTATION	rush
PITHY	meaning
GALVANIZE	quicken
IMPIOUS	unite
ADMONISH	word history

Greek Salad
Serves 4

Salad:
1 large English cucumber
2 medium vine tomatoes
1 small red onion
¾ cup whole, pitted Kalamata olives
8 oz feta cheese

Dressing:
2 tbsp red wine vinegar
2 tbsp extra virgin olive oil
Salt and freshly ground black pepper to taste

Peel the cucumber. Quarter it lengthwise and chop it into ½" chunks. Thinly slice the onion and chop the tomatoes into ½" chunks.

Dice the cheese into ¼" chunks.

Combine the vegetables and olives in a bowl.

In a separate bowl, whisk together the oil, vinegar, and a pinch of salt and pepper. Drizzle the dressing over the vegetables.

Add the feta cheese and gently toss to prevent the feta from crumbling.

Serve.

There's nothing MONOTONE about a Greek salad, also known as a "RUSTIC salad." The colorful ingredients, DISPARATE textures and sharp odor UNIFY to SCINTILLATE the senses. Feta is an aged, PREDOMINANTLY sheep's milk cheese that is ripened in BRINE. It is roughly MEDIAL on the SPECTRUM of soft and hard cheeses, having qualities of both. Add more Kalamata olives if you have a PREFERENCE for salt.

MONOTONE	range
RUSTIC	saltwater
DISPARATE	middle
UNIFY	choice
SCINTILLATE	unite
PREDOMINANT	spark
BRINE	rural
MEDIAL	sameness
SPECTRUM	unequal
PREFERENCE	overriding

Watermelon, Feta, and Tomato Salad
Serves 4

Salad:
½ small watermelon
8 oz feta cheese
1 large Roma tomato

Dressing:
½ cup balsamic vinegar
1 tbsp extra virgin olive oil
3 tsp sugar
1 garlic clove
Salt and freshly ground black pepper to taste

Remove the watermelon rind and chop it and the feta cheese into ½" thick squares.

Slice the tomato into 4 even pieces.

Crush the garlic or mince it finely.

Cook the balsamic vinegar, garlic, and sugar in a small pot on a medium heat. Stir occasionally, until the mixture has reduced by half. This should take a few minutes.

Stack a slice of watermelon, a slice of cheese, and a slice of tomato into a tower-like structure on a plate. Pour ¼ of the balsamic vinegar on each of the 4 plates, sprinkle with salt and pepper, and add ¼ of the olive oil onto each tower.

Serve immediately.

*Tip: Add a mound of watercress to each plate for a spicy kick.

Can you PROFFER a CONJECTURE as to the source of the name, "watermelon"? This juicy DELICACY is 92% water, hence the APPELLATION (duh!). No PREVARICATION here! Contrary to popular opinion, watermelon is a vegetable, not a fruit, and every part of it, including the rind, is EDIBLE. China is the number one PURVEYOR of this healthy treat, which ORIGINATED in the Kalahari Desert in Africa. Watermelon is NUTRITIVE and may promote LONGEVITY.

PROFFER	supplier
CONJECTURE	nourishing
DELICACY	began
APPELLATION	resilience
PREVARICATION	guess
EDIBLE	offer
PURVEYOR	deception
ORIGINATED	name
NUTRITIVE	consumable
LONGEVITY	fine food

Lima Bean And Cilantro Salad
Serves 3

Salad:
1 (15.5) oz can of lima beans
2 tbsp minced fresh cilantro leaves

Dressing:
1 tbsp lemon juice
1 tbsp extra virgin olive oil
Salt and freshly ground black pepper to taste

Rinse, drain and pat dry the lima beans.

Mix the lima beans and cilantro in a small bowl.

In a separate bowl, whisk together the lemon juice and oil. Drizzle over the top of the lima beans and cilantro. Sprinkle with salt and pepper. Mix well, gently, so as to not purée the beans.

Serve.

A loose CONFEDERACY of members of the website ihatecilantro.com are united in their IRREPRESSIBLE ODIUM for cilantro, an herb they consider to be the "PLEBIAN parsley." They VILIFY its taste, CHASTISE any restaurant that serves it and spew VENOM about every aspect of this feathery leaf. You may not agree with their ongoing HARANGUE, but you have to admire their CANDOR and INEXHAUSTIBLE conviction.

———

CONFEDERACY	common
IRREPRESSIBLE	honesty
ODIUM	poison
PLEBIAN	unlimited
VILIFY	criticism
CHASTISE	uncontrollable
VENOM	league
HARANGUE	slander
CANDOR	criticize
INEXHAUSTIBLE	dislike

Black Bean And Corn Salad
Serves 3

Salad:
1 (15.5 oz) can black beans
2 ears corn
1 small red onion
1 small bell pepper, any color
1½ tbsp minced fresh cilantro leaves
¾ cup water

Dressing:
1 lemon, juiced
2 tbsp extra virgin olive oil
Salt and freshly ground black pepper to taste

Drain, rinse and pat dry the beans. Cut the kernels off of the corn.
Dice the onion and bell pepper.

Cook the corn kernels in the water, in a small pot on a high heat, covered, for 6 minutes.
Drain and allow them to cool completely.

Combine the corn, beans, onion, bell pepper, and cilantro in a bowl.

In a separate bowl, whisk together the oil, lemon juice, and salt and pepper.
Drizzle over the bean and corn salad.

Serve.

The DENIZENS of Mexico were the first to harvest corn as their VOCATION, and the crop has since experienced ROBUST growth. The DIVERSE, colorful SPECIES include ASHEN yellow or ALABASTER, and TINTS of black and red. Over time, the growth in popularity of other types has BURGEONED. Corn is used in a variety of everyday foods. Pancakes and eggs have to beware of the CEREAL killer!

DENIZEN	powerful
VOCATION	group
ROBUST	white
DIVERSE	hue
SPECIES	grow
ASHEN	inhabitant
ALABASTER	grain
TINT	various
BURGEON	pale
CEREAL	job

Wedge Salad
Serves 4

Salad:
1 iceberg lettuce
1 medium vine tomato
1 small red onion
4 slices bacon

Dressing:
¾ cup plain Greek yogurt
¼ cup buttermilk
1 tbsp white vinegar
½ tsp Worcestershire sauce
½ cup crumbled blue cheese
Salt and freshly ground black pepper to taste

For the dressing: combine all of the ingredients.

For the salad: cut the lettuce into quarters. Dice the tomato. Chop the onion into small chunks. Cook the bacon on a medium – high heat for 2 – 3 minutes on each side. Blot with paper towels to remove the excess fat. Crumble the bacon.

Drizzle the desired amount of dressing on each lettuce wedge.

Top with tomatoes, onions and crumbled bacon bits.

Serve.

A wedge salad threatens DOMESTIC TRANQUILITY in an episode of the television series *Modern Family*. The IMBROGLIO involves a wife who, by trying to SIMPLIFY the task of making dinner, IMPELS her spouse toward PALPABLE anger. The wedge salad is the TRAMMEL that first IMPEDES RATIONALISM, but, because it's Hollywood, won't be allowed to destroy the family WEAL. They will live happily ever after.

DOMESTIC	tangible
TRANQUILITY	entanglement
IMBROGLIO	calm
SIMPLIFY	well-being
IMPEL	hinder
PALPABLE	impediment
TRAMMEL	drive
IMPEDE	make easier
RATIONALISM	household
WEAL	reason

Fig And Olive Tapenade On Baked Baguette
Makes about 20 slices of baguette

7 oz dried golden figs
6.5 oz pitted Kalamata olives
½ cup extra virgin olive oil
1 tsp black pepper
1 baguette

Preheat the oven to 375° Fahrenheit.

In a food processor or blender, process the figs, olives, oil, and pepper until the mixture becomes a paste. Set aside.

Slice a baguette into ¾" thick rounds. One baguette should make about 20 slices. Place the bread slices on a large sheet pan and bake for about 12 - 15 minutes. Spread the tapenade on the bread.

Serve.

*Tip: Extra tapenade can be refrigerated for future use.

Tapenade is a paste that can be used as a condiment, or more commonly, paired with bread to WHET the appetite and INITIATE a meal. Olive, the FUNDAMENTAL COMPONENT, is mashed into a spread with oil and capers. Add figs to TANTALIZE the taste buds and PROPEL the PALATE on a TRAJECTORY from the PROSAIC to the sublime. There will be no need to COERCE your guests into asking for seconds!

WHET	bully
INITIATE	stimulate
FUNDAMENTAL	path
COMPONENT	push
TANTALIZE	appetite
PROPEL	begin
PALATE	excite
TRAJECTORY	basic
PROSAIC	part
COERCE	commonplace

Smoked Salmon, Cucumber, And Cream Cheese On Baguette
Makes about 12 slices

½ baguette
12 tsp cream cheese
1 tbsp capers
½ cucumber
12 small slices smoked salmon
3 tbsp extra virgin olive oil
Freshly ground black pepper to taste

Cut the baguette into ½" thick slices.

Peel and thinly slice the cucumber, making approximately 24 slices.

Preheat a grill pan or regular sauté pan to a medium - high heat.

Drizzle the baguette slices with half of the oil on each side. Place on the pan and cook for about 3 - 4 minutes on each side.

Meanwhile, stir the capers and cream cheese together.

Once the baguette slices are done, evenly spread about 1 tsp of the cream cheese and caper mixture on each slice. Top with 2 slices of cucumber and 1 slice of smoked salmon. Finish with black pepper.

Serve.

It takes an ICONOCLAST to serve this dish, a FUSION of eastern and western European fare. New Yorkers at your Sunday brunch will be APPALLED by the DISREGARD for tradition. Your FEALTY for the SUBSTANTIVE, beloved bagel has been abandoned for a SYLPH? Remain DAUNTLESS even if your guests LOATHE the loaf! The skinny on the baguette, a symbol of French culture, is that a crispy crust and chewy middle matched with lox and cream cheese promise a GRATIFYING twist on a classic favorite.

ICONOCLAST	slender being
FUSION	loyalty
APPALL	satisfy
DISREGARD	shock
FEALTY	mixture
SUBSTANTIVE	fearless
SYLPH	hate
DAUNTLESS	solid
LOATHE	rebel
GRATIFY	neglect

Pea And Prosciutto Soup
Serves 4 - 5

2 cups low sodium broth, any type
1 lb frozen peas
1 large shallot
1 small leek
1 tbsp unsalted butter
1 tbsp extra virgin olive oil
4 sprigs mint
¼ - ½ cup heavy cream
4 tbsp sour cream
2 slices prosciutto
Salt and freshly ground black pepper to taste

Mince (separately) the shallot, mint and prosciutto. Mince only the white and light green parts of the leek.

Heat the butter and oil in a large pot on a medium heat. Add the shallots and leek and cook for about 3 minutes, stirring occasionally. Add the broth, peas, salt and pepper, and ¾ of the mint. Cook on a medium heat for about 5 minutes. Transfer to a blender or food processor and blend until smooth, while slowly pouring in the heavy cream. Ladle into soup bowls.

In a separate bowl, mix together the sour cream, the remaining mint, and the prosciutto. Dollop 1 tbsp of the mixture into each soup bowl.

Serve immediately.

Curing is an ancient technique for food PRESERVATION and flavoring. TYPICALLY, meat or fish are SUBJECTED to treatment with salt, sugar, nitrates, nitrate, smoking, or some combination thereof. Salting meat prevents it from becoming RANCID, the addition of sugar encourages BENEFICIAL bacteria to REPRODUCE, and nitrates and nitrite impart a ruddy TINGE. Prosciutto, the Italian salt-cured ham, is thoroughly DESICCATED during a PROLONGED process that can take two years. The finished product is a staple in the kitchen of any serious GOURMAND.

PRESERVATION	breed
TYPICAL	useful
SUBJECTED	normal
RANCID	connoisseur
BENEFICIAL	lengthen
REPRODUCE	tint
TINGE	put through
DESICCATE	rotten
PROLONG	dry
GOURMAND	conservation

Potage Parmentier (Potato Leek Soup)
Serves 6 - 8

5 Yukon gold potatoes (4 – 5 cups when chopped)
2 – 3 medium leeks (4 cups when chopped)
4 cups water
⅛ cup chives
½ cup heavy cream
1½ - 2 cups whole milk
3 tbsp unsalted butter
Salt and freshly ground black pepper to taste

Peel and chop the potatoes into 1" chunks. Chop the whites of the leeks into 1" chunks. Chop the chives into small pieces.

Bring the water to a boil in a large pot. Add the potatoes and leeks and cover. Cook them for about 20 minutes or until the vegetables are tender. Drain the water.

Transfer the potatoes and leeks to a food processor or blender. Add the chives, heavy cream, whole milk and butter, and season to taste. Process until smooth.

Return the soup to the large pot and cook on high for a few minutes, stirring, or until the soup reaches your desired temperature.

Serve.

The EXPATRIATE Julia Child, an ADROIT chef, included Potage Parmentier in the famous, "Mastering The Art Of French Cooking." The recipe was the first one in her book, a TESTAMENT to its importance. Julia's COMMENTARY on cooking TECHNIQUE offered INSIGHT to tricks of the trade. Trying to MIMIC her work is a task TANTAMOUNT to reaching for perfection, since most people can't ASPIRE to achieve an IOTA of her talent.

EXPATRIATE	equivalent
ADROIT	imitate
TESTAMENT	speck
COMMENTARY	perceptiveness
TECHNIQUE	skillful
INSIGHT	method
MIMIC	aim
TANTAMOUNT	evidence
ASPIRE	explanation
IOTA	emigrant

Corn Chowder
Serves 5

4 ears corn
2 medium Idaho potatoes
1 medium white onion
2 cups whole milk
5 cups broth, your choice
½ cup grated cheddar cheese + extra for garnishing
5 slices bacon
2 tbsp unsalted butter
2 tbsp extra virgin olive oil
Salt and freshly ground black pepper to taste

Cut off the corn kernels by sliding a knife down the side of the corn. Peel the potatoes. Chop the potatoes and onions into small chunks.

In a large pot on low, heat the butter and oil. Add the onions, a pinch of salt and pepper, and cook for about 15 minutes, stirring occasionally. Add the broth, milk, corn kernels, and potatoes. Bring the mixture to a boil, stir, cover, reduce the heat to low and cook for about 20 minutes. Stir in the ½ cup of cheese until just melted.

In a pan on a medium - high heat, cook the bacon on each side for a few minutes or until golden brown. Garnish the soup with crumbled bacon and grated cheddar cheese.

Serve.

A PRODIGIOUS amount of corn, also ALLUDED to as "MAIZE," is PROPAGATED in the American ACREAGE. KERNELS of this vegetable, joined with potatoes, make cooking this soup PRACTICABLE. Chowder, a PONDEROUS milk stew, offers a TANGIBLE meal that is tasty, but may be a HAZARD to your health.

PRODIGIOUS	feasible
ALLUDE	weighty
MAIZE	touchable
PROPAGATE	danger
ACREAGE	spread
KERNEL	land
PRACTICABLE	refer
PONDEROUS	corn
TANGIBLE	immense
HAZARD	nugget

Chicken And Dumpling Soup
Serves 8-10

Broth:
1 whole (2 lbs) chicken
3 stalks celery
17 baby carrots
1 small white onion
18 cups water
1½ tsp pepper + extra to taste
1 tsp dried rosemary
1 tsp dried parsley
1 tsp dried thyme
1 tbsp garlic salt
1 tbsp seasoning mix
Regular kosher salt to taste

Dumplings:
4 tbsp unsalted butter
1 cup milk
2 eggs
1 cup flour
¼ tsp nutmeg
½ tsp salt

Divide the celery in half lengthwise. Chop the celery and carrots into ¼" chunks. Chop the onion into small chunks.

Put the chicken, water, garlic salt, pepper, and herbs in a large stockpot. Bring to a boil, cover, and cook for 30 minutes, stirring occasionally. Add the vegetables and cook for another 30 minutes, stirring occasionally. Turn off the heat and remove the chicken from the pot.

Allow the chicken to cool and then shred with 2 forks into bite size pieces. Place back in the pot and cook on a high heat for about 15 minutes and then turn to a low heat once you are ready to cook the dumplings.

Meanwhile, heat the butter and milk on a low heat in a small saucepan. Add the flour, and slowly whisk in the eggs, nutmeg and salt until just combined. Use 2 spoons to scoop the dumplings into the pot. If making small dumplings (about 1 - 2 tsp each), cook covered for about 3 minutes. If making large dumplings (about 1 tbsp each), cook covered for about 6 minutes. You will know when the dumplings are ready when a knife inserted easily slides into the soft dumpling.

Serve.

Dumplings are part of the Chinese New Year REGALIA because they symbolize ABUNDANT riches. This celebration marks the one time of the year that those in PENURY defy SUBSISTENCE living and join the SOLVENT, eating as well as the WELL-TO-DO. Dumplings are also served when families REUNITE for memorable occasions and to offer a special "ADIEU." They are also SIGNIFICANT in many other cultures where they are appreciated for their taste without being a measure of SUCCESS.

REGALIA	poverty
ABUNDANT	survival
PENURY	prosperous
SUBSISTENCE	important
SOLVENT	rejoin
WELL-TO-DO	goodbye
REUNITE	accomplishment
ADIEU	royal emblems
SIGNIFICANT	plentiful
SUCCESS	debt-free

Gazpacho
Serves 4-5

1 large English cucumber (3⅓ cups when cubed)
3 small vine tomatoes (3 cups when cubed)
2 large peppers, green and red (3⅓ cups when cubed)
1 small red onion (1½ cups when cubed)
2 tsp minced garlic
1 lime, juiced
2 cups tomato juice
1 cup white vinegar
⅓ cup extra virgin olive oil
Salt and freshly ground black pepper to taste

Chop the cucumber lengthwise and then into small cubes with the skin on. Cube the tomatoes, peppers and onion.

Combine all of the ingredients in a large bowl and mix well. Cover with plastic wrap and refrigerate for at least 2 hours.

Serve cold.

Gazpacho ASCRIBES the BIBULOUS with credit for two food groups because this soup qualifies as an AQUEOUS *salad*. It's a CORNUCOPIA of nutrition with ENORMOUS health benefits. This Spanish MASTERPIECE was popular before and after the DISCOVERY of The New World, and can be altered in surprising ways to EMBODY your taste. Don't BELITTLE stale bread! The use of old bread and vegetables is EXCUSABLE in making gazpacho.

ASCRIBE	water
BIBULOUS	outstanding work
AQUEOUS	denigrate
CORNUCOPIA	huge
ENORMOUS	attribute
MASTERPIECE	pardonable
DISCOVERY	abundance
EMBODY	fond of drinking
BELITTLE	manifest
EXCUSABLE	finding

Brussels Sprouts And Mushroom Tart
Serves 6

1 large Portobello mushroom
8 Brussels sprouts
⅛ cup balsamic vinegar
2 tbsp unsalted butter
1 sheet store bought puff pastry
1 tbsp grated Parmesan cheese
Salt and freshly ground black pepper to taste
Nonstick cooking spray

Preheat the oven to 375° Fahrenheit.

Clean the Portobello mushroom with a damp paper town and dice into small chunks. Thinly slice the Brussels sprouts. Defrost the puff pastry.

Melt the butter in a pan on a medium heat. Add the mushroom, Brussels sprouts, balsamic vinegar, and salt and pepper to taste. Cook for 5 - 6 minutes or until the vegetables become tender.

Lightly spray a sheet pan with nonstick cooking spray. To assemble the tart, lay the puff pastry sheet on the pan and cut the edges off to make it round. Score the pastry using a fork, leaving a 1" border around the perimeter. Spoon the cooked vegetable mixture onto the center of the puff pastry. Fold over the puff pastry to encase the vegetables and make a border. Gently pinch to form pleats and secure the dough. Make sure to leave an opening at the top where you can see the vegetables. Sprinkle Parmesan cheese on the vegetables and bake for about 30 minutes. If the cheese starts to brown too much, place a circle of tin foil over the vegetables.

Allow the tart to cool for at least 8 minutes before serving.

A large BEVY of mushrooms, many of them poisonous, have existed on earth since far back in ANTIQUITY. Eating the most NONDESCRIPT mushroom can have DIRE consequences. The ONUS is on you to familiarize yourself with features of DELETERIOUS species and to remain VIGILANT when gathering wild mushrooms. To avoid a KNOTTY situation, it may be PRUDENT to confine your fungus-hunting to the local market. Mushrooms and Brussels sprouts are an ECLECTIC combination that pleases every time.

BEVY	burden
ANTIQUITY	dreadful
NONDESCRIPT	complicated
DIRE	diverse
ONUS	cluster
DELETERIOUS	cautious
VIGILANT	past
KNOTTY	indescribable
PRUDENT	alert
ECLECTIC	harmful

Pear And Gorgonzola Tart
Serves 6

2 medium ripe Bosc pears
2½ tbsp unsalted butter
1 tbsp sugar
2 - 3 tbsp crumbled Gorgonzola cheese
1 sheet store bought puff pastry
Nonstick cooking spray

Preheat the oven to 400° Fahrenheit.

Peel and thinly slice the pears into 1" long strips. Place them in a pan on a medium heat, add the butter and sugar and cook for 10 minutes or until the pears become tender and golden brown. Remove from the heat and let rest.

Spray a sheet pan with nonstick cooking spray. To assemble the tart, lay the puff pastry sheet on the sheet pan and cut the edges off to make it round. Using a fork, score the pastry in the center, leaving a 1" border around the perimeter. Place the pears onto the scored fork marks and top with Gorgonzola cheese. Fold over the puff pastry to encase the filling and make a border. Gently pinch to form pleats and secure the dough.

Bake for 20 - 25 minutes or until the crust is golden brown and flaky, and the cheese is melted.

Serve warm.

The NOXIOUS odor of Gorgonzola can INTIMIDATE even the most INTREPID foodie. Anyone with an AVERSION to blue mold might BALK at sampling this whole milk cheese, which DERIVES its VARIEGATED, marble pattern from the growth of Penicillium spores. The brave will be rewarded! The SAVORY taste and crumbly texture are TEMPERED by the soft, sweet pear, making this dish delightfully PALATABLE.

NOXIOUS	obtain
INTIMIDATE	tangy
INTREPID	refuse
AVERSION	tasty
BALK	fearless
DERIVE	neutralized
VARIEGATED	dislike
SAVORY	frighten
TEMPERED	unpleasant
PALATABLE	different

Sylvia's Steamed Cabbage With Caraway And Ground "Meat"
Serves 5-6

1 medium Savoy cabbage
14 oz ground meat or vegan meatless "meat"
2 tbsp oil (any kind)
2 tsp whole caraway seeds
2 cups low sodium broth (any kind)
Salt and freshly ground black pepper to taste

Chop the cabbage into thin strips.

Heat the oil in a large pot on a medium heat. Add the meatless "meat" or ground meat and separate it into medium size chunks with the back of a wooden spoon.

Add the caraway seeds, and a pinch of salt and pepper and cook for about 4 minutes, stirring occasionally, or until golden brown.

Add the cabbage and broth and cook on a low heat with the cover on for about 50 minutes, stirring occasionally. Salt to taste.

Serve.

There are various uses of "cabbage" in the common VERNACULAR. On the streets of England and Russia, "cabbage" implies cash RESOURCES. In the U.S., "cabbage head" CONFERS the unflattering description of a BUFFOON, someone who is INANE or altogether VAPID, the type of person who considers caraway a seed, when in fact it's a fruit. The German translation of cabbage is used to cast an ASPERSION on an EXECRABLE individual, a form of MOCKERY. It may be more SAGACIOUS to focus on the positive side of cabbage and caraway by just enjoying this tasty dish!

———

VERNACULAR	ridicule
RESOURCE	stupid
CONFER	wise
BUFFOON	dull
INANE	clown
VAPID	grant
ASPERSION	supply
EXECRABLE	everyday language
MOCKERY	slander
SAGACIOUS	abominable

Nancy's Hummus With Pita Chips
Serves 8

Hummus:
1 (16 oz) can of chickpeas
¾ cup tahini
½ cup water
3 tbsp lemon juice
3 tbsp Tabasco sauce
2 tsp garlic powder
½ tsp cumin
¼ tsp paprika
½ tsp salt + extra to taste
2 tbsp extra virgin olive oil

Pita Chips:
2 pita pockets
1 tbsp extra virgin olive oil

For the hummus: rinse the chickpeas well and soak in water for 20 minutes. During this time, change the water twice and drain well.

Process the chickpeas in a food processor until finely chopped. Gradually add the water and process until almost smooth (slightly granular). Add the cumin, garlic powder, ½ tsp salt, Tabasco sauce, and lemon juice. Process until it is just mixed. Add the tahini and pulse until smooth. Chill.

When ready to serve, place in a bowl, sprinkle with paprika and drizzle with 2 tbsp of olive oil.

For the pita chips: cut each pita pocket into 8 pie slices. Place on a baking sheet and drizzle with 1 tbsp of olive oil and a pinch of salt. Bake them at 400° Fahrenheit for 6 – 8 minutes or until crispy.

Place a dollop of hummus on each pita chip.

Serve.

Hummus is a chickpea mash that occupies the center of a clash over ownership. In 2008, LOBBYISTS for the Association of Lebanese Industrialists requested protected status from the European Commission, asking permission to CHARACTERIZE hummus as a UNIQUELY Lebanese dish. This RANCOROUS action was PROVOCATIVE, causing other Middle Eastern producers of hummus to CONTRAVENE, each claiming their own version as EXEMPLARY. WARY bloggers immediately moved to DISCREDIT the claim, which the Lebanese could not SUBSTANTIATE.

LOBBYIST	obstruct
CHARACTERIZE	person influencing legislators
UNIQUE	dishonor
RANCOR	a model
PROVOCATIVE	one of a kind
CONTRAVENE	stimulating
EXEMPLARY	validate
WARY	bitterness
DISCREDIT	describe
SUBSTANTIATE	cautious

Onion Casserole
Serves 4 - 5

3 medium Vidalia onions
1 (10¾ oz) can cream of mushroom soup
¼ cup sour cream
½ cup milk
2 cups crushed potato chips
1½ cups shredded sharp cheddar cheese
Salt and freshly ground black pepper to taste

Preheat the oven to 375° Fahrenheit.

Have an 8" x 8" pan ready.

Thinly slice the Vidalia onions and separate them into rings.

Combine the cream of mushroom soup, onions, sour cream, milk, and a pinch of salt and pepper in a large bowl. Mix well.

Place about ⅓ of the mixture in the pan. Top with ⅓ of the cheddar cheese, and ⅓ of the chips. Repeat this process 2 more times.

Cover with tin foil and bake for about 1 hour.

Serve.

A person encountering you sobbing at the cutting board might question your EQUANIMITY if the STIMULUS of your visible GRIEF, an onion, was not APPARENT. Cutting an onion releases a VOLATILE gas that mixes with water in your eye, forming sulfuric acid, an IRRITANT that causes UNAVOIDABLE tears to form. You can SUBMERGE the onion in water while cutting it, or refrigerate it in advance to DEPRESS its temperature, both of which will cause your tear glands to become QUIESCENT.

EQUANIMITY	distress
STIMULUS	sink
GRIEF	inevitable
APPARENT	annoyance
VOLATILE	lower
IRRITANT	inspiration
UNAVOIDABLE	unstable
SUBMERGE	inactive
DEPRESS	obvious
QUIESCENT	composure

Latkes (Potato Pancakes)
Makes 14 latkes

1 lb Idaho potatoes
½ cup minced white onion
1 egg, beaten
1 tbsp minced parsley
½ tsp pepper
½ cup vegetable oil + more if needed
½ tsp salt + more to taste
Sour cream or applesauce as a topping (optional)

Peel and grate the potatoes and soak in cold water for 2 minutes.

Remove the grated potatoes from the water and use a clean kitchen towel to ring out all of the water. Transfer to a bowl with the egg, onion, parsley and pepper. Mix well.

Place half of the oil in a large pan and set on a medium - high heat. Add half of the potato mixture, in rounds of 2 tbsp. Slightly press down with a spatula.

Cook for about 5 minutes on each side and transfer to a plate lined with paper towels. Pat to dry the excess oil. Salt to taste.

Add the rest of the oil with the second batch of latkes and repeat the above process.

Serve.

*Tip: Latkes are traditionally served with applesauce or sour cream.

Latkes, traditionally served during the Jewish FÊTE of Hanukkah, consist of shredded potatoes fried in oil. Eggs support the INTEGRITY of the patty, which is KNEADED to RESEMBLE a hamburger. Shredded zucchini or sweet potatoes can be used to DEVIATE from the standard recipe. Latkes COMMEMORATE the PREDICAMENT of the Maccabees, a warrior group who SALVAGED a MINUTE amount of oil that should have lasted for one day, bur miraculously burned for eight. This story continues to CAPTIVATE the minds of young children.

FÊTE	honor
INTEGRITY	celebration
KNEAD	save
RESEMBLE	enrapture
DEVIATE	massage
COMMEMORATE	parallel
PREDICAMENT	wholeness
SALVAGE	plight
MINUTE	trifling
CAPTIVATE	diverge

Steamed Bok Choy With Collard Greens
Serves 3

2 small bok choy
3 large collard green leaves
1 small white onion
¼ cup broth, any type
1 tbsp unsalted butter
1 tbsp extra virgin olive oil
1 tbsp low sodium soy sauce
1 tbsp oyster sauce
Salt and freshly ground black pepper to taste

Remove the stems and leaves from the core of the bok choy, keeping them intact. Chop the collard greens into medium strips. Mince the onion.

Heat the butter and oil in a large pot on a medium heat. Add the onion and cook for about 3 minutes, stirring occasionally.

Add the bok choy, collard greens, and a pinch of salt and pepper. Cook on a high heat for about 1 - 2 minutes. Reduce the heat to low and add the broth, oyster sauce, and soy sauce. Cook covered, for about 6 minutes.

Serve.

Bok choy is composed of a bulb and greens that are DISSIMILAR in texture. The bulb is TREMENDOUSLY crunchy, while the greens are delicate. The plant itself is NEUTER because it's unisex. Bok choy can be made into kimchi, a Korean DELECTATION, or join a CONCORD of pickled vegetables, all of which can set your mouth AFIRE. This vegetable may be eaten after finishing evening ABLUTIONS as many studies suggest that it causes DROWSINESS. It's important to thoroughly wash and SUPERFICIALLY DISINFECT this Chinese cabbage with cold water before eating.

DISSIMILAR	clean
TREMENDOUS	sleepy
NEUTER	surface
DELECTATION	different
CONCORD	sexless
AFIRE	harmony
ABLUTION	burning
DROWSY	delight
SUPERFICIAL	wonderful
DISINFECT	washing

Fried Green Tomatoes
Serves 4 - 6

4 green tomatoes
¼ cup cornmeal
½ cup flour
3 eggs
3 tbsp buttermilk
3 tbsp sparkling water
½ tsp cayenne pepper
1 cup panko bread crumbs
Vegetable oil
Salt and freshly ground black pepper to taste

Chop the tomatoes into ½" rounds.

In a dish, combine the flour, cornmeal, cayenne, and a pinch of salt and pepper.

In another dish, combine the eggs, buttermilk and sparkling water.

Have another dish ready with the panko.

For the fried green tomatoes: fill a saucepan almost ½ way up with oil and place it on a medium heat. Dredge the tomatoes in the flour mixture, then dip them in the egg mixture, and then into the panko. Place them in the pan and cook for a few minutes on each side. Once golden brown on each side, pat dry with a paper towel, and lightly salt.

Serve.

The 1991 film, "Fried Green Tomatoes," is a PROTOTYPE of COMICAL movies with a dark side. Fried green tomatoes are part of Southern FOLKLORE and the film helped EMBOLDEN many to try an EATABLE version of unripe food. Panko, a type of Japanese breadcrumb, is GENERALLY made from bread without crust. The crumbs are dusted on the green tomatoes before they become FLORID and are important in order to GENERATE a good crunch factor. This tasty treat will EXCEED your expectations and GLADDEN your Southern friends.

PROTOTYPE	produce
COMICAL	red
FOLKLORE	model
EMBOLDEN	surpass
EATABLE	mainly
GENERALLY	palatable
FLORID	encourage
GENERATE	delight
EXCEED	tales
GLADDEN	funny

Roasted Red Peppers
Serves 4

4 medium, whole red bell peppers
2 tbsp extra virgin olive oil
Salt and freshly ground black pepper to taste

Preheat the oven to 375° Fahrenheit.

Cut the top off of the peppers and remove the seeds and vertebrae.

Place the peppers on a small baking dish, top down. Drizzle ½ tbsp of olive oil on each pepper and sprinkle with salt. Mix well with clean hands.

Place in the oven and bake for about 1 hour or until the skin is charred.

Once done, place the peppers in a glass bowl and cover tightly with tin foil. Allow the roasted peppers to sit for at least 20 minutes.

Remove the skin and serve with a pinch of salt and pepper.

Upon returning to Europe following his NOMADIC life in the New World, Christopher Columbus brought back a strange looking red fruit as a MEMENTO of his experience. The EMINENT explorer REFERRED to this oddity as the "pepper." During that time, peppercorns were RENOWNED as a prized spice from India, which only the AFFLUENT could afford. Why Columbus chose to name his fruit after the spice is an unanswered question that continues to CONFOUND historians. Today, the red pepper still is widely known by Columbus' NOMENCLATURE and as the "bell pepper." Peppers are CULTIVATED in MYRIAD colors, including red, yellow, green, orange, purple, and rainbow.

———

NOMADIC	respected
MEMENTO	wandering
EMINENT	grow
REFER	name
RENOWN	wealthy
AFFLUENT	confuse
CONFOUND	mention
NOMENCLATURE	many
CULTIVATE	souvenir
MYRIAD	fame

Spicy Stewed Potatoes
Serves 4 - 5

24 oz fingerling potatoes
1 small white onion (about 1 cup when chopped)
1 small red bell pepper (about 1 cup when sliced)
2 cups low sodium chicken broth
3 tsp tomato paste
½ tsp chipotle pepper flakes
Extra virgin olive oil
Salt and freshly ground black pepper to taste

Chop the onion and slice the pepper, each thinly.

Drizzle the bottom of a large pot with olive oil and place on a medium heat. Add the onions and peppers, cook for 5 minutes, stirring occasionally until the vegetables are soft and golden. Add the potatoes, stir, and cook for 5 minutes, stirring occasionally. Next, add the chipotle pepper flakes, salt, pepper, tomato paste and chicken stock.

Stir, cover, and cook for 30 minutes, stirring occasionally until the potatoes are fork tender.

Serve the potatoes with the sauce on top.

The Irish potato famine of 1845 killed in EXCESS of one million people and caused one QUARTER of the POPULACE to EMIGRATE, fleeing for safety to other countries. At the time, potatoes were the QUINTESSENTIAL Irish food, a lower and middle class staple. The ASSAILANT, a potato fungus, DISSEMINATED rapidly, ULTIMATELY ERADICATING the entire crop. The ANNIHILATION of Irish potatoes is legendary in the history of Ireland.

EXCESS	typical
QUARTER	destroy
POPULACE	destruction
EMIGRATE	finally
QUINTESSENTIAL	spread
ASSAILANT	resettle
DISSEMINATE	one fourth
ULTIMATELY	inhabitants
ERADICATE	attacker
ANNIHILATION	superfluous

Glazed Carrots
Serves 2 - 3

35 baby carrots
1 tbsp unsalted butter
½ cup no pulp orange juice
2 tbsp packed light brown sugar

Add all of the ingredients to a pot, stir, and cook, covered, on a low heat for about 15 minutes.

Remove from the heat, remove the cover, and let sit for about 5 minutes to allow the sauce to slightly thicken.

Serve warm.

Caramelization is a cooking method that chefs use for sweetening, in order to offer "good RIDDANCE" to bitter foods. Caramelization occurs when sugar changes chemically due to high temperature. It seems like RIGMAROLE, but to achieve the perfect "caramel," a SERVICEABLE pan and a COURAGEOUS DEMEANOR are needed. It would not be MENDACIOUS to say that this technique takes DEXTERITY, COMPOSURE and acceptance of the risk of SEVERE COSMETIC burns.

RIDDANCE	intense
RIGAMAROLE	untrue
SERVICEABLE	conduct
COURAGEOUS	deliverance from
DEMEANOR	brave
MENDACIOUS	usable
DEXTERITY	external
COMPOSURE	skill
SEVERE	calm
COSMETIC	nonsense

Asparagus With Hollandaise Sauce
Serves 3

Asparagus:
1½ lbs asparagus
Extra virgin olive oil
Salt and freshly ground black pepper to taste

Hollandaise Sauce:
2 egg yolks
2½ tbsp lemon juice
⅛ tsp cayenne pepper
4 tbsp unsalted butter
¼ tsp salt

Preheat the oven to 375° Fahrenheit.

For the Hollandaise sauce: whisk together the egg yolks, lemon juice, salt, and cayenne until slightly thickened (about 1 minute). Set aside.

Melt the butter in a small saucepan on a medium heat. Slowly stir the melted butter into the egg yolk mixture. Be careful to do this very slowly so as to not scramble the eggs.

Place the mixture back in the saucepan and cook on a low heat for 1 minute, whisking continuously until the sauce thickens.

For the asparagus: peel and break off the ends where they naturally snap. Place the asparagus on a sheet pan and drizzle with olive oil and sprinkle with salt and pepper. Bake in the oven for about 20 minutes. The baking time depends on the thickness of the asparagus.

Serve the asparagus spears with the hollandaise sauce.

Hollandaise sauce is considered to be an ACCLAIMED "mother sauce" of France. This TEPID emulsion of egg yolks, butter, salt, pepper, and lemon juice makes a creamy and LUSTROUS topping for vegetables, meats, and CROISSANTS. Four other ARTISAN crafted tried-and-trues are considered to be KIN to hollandaise. There are a few LOWLY and UNBECOMING qualities of hollandaise served over asparagus. The dish can be a natural LAXATIVE and make urine NOISOME.

ACCLAIM	French butter roll
TEPID	craftsperson
LUSTROUS	praise
CROISSANT	shining
ARTISAN	warm
KIN	unattractive
LOWLY	relation
UNBECOMING	humble
LAXATIVE	malodorous
NOISOME	bowel stimulant

Brown Rice With Almonds And Raisins
Serves 4

2½ cups + 2 tbsp water or broth
1 cup brown rice
½ cup mixed raisins
½ cup slivered almonds
1 tbsp oil (any kind)
1 tsp salt + extra to taste

Heat the broth or water in a medium pot on a high heat until it boils. In a bowl, mix the rice and oil to prevent sticking. Add the rice, cover, and bring to a low simmer. Cook for about 25 - 30 minutes or until all of the water is absorbed.

Let the rice sit in the pan while plumping the raisins.

To plump the raisins, microwave them with 2 tbsp of water (or broth) for about 30 seconds.

Add the plumped raisins and slivered almonds to the rice. Fluff with a fork and salt to taste.

Serve.

Brown rice, a more PUDGY, nutty and hearty version of white rice, is similar in carbohydrates and protein but has more nutritive value. The light AUBURN rice is produced by removing the husk, its UPPERMOST layer. Rice is harvested, sometimes using a SCYTHE, then packaged and sold in SUPERNUMERARY and TITANIC PLENITUDE. The preferred color choice of rice is in FLUX, but white REFUSES to surrender the lead. PERHAPS in the future, this will change.

––––––

PUDGY	abundance
AUBURN	huge
UPPERMOST	decline
SCYTHE	plump
SUPERNUMERARY	outer
TITANIC	excessive
PLENITUDE	change
FLUX	tawny
REFUSE	maybe
PERHAPS	tool

Fried Plantains
Serves 1 – 2 (about 12 slices)

1 ripe plantain
¼ cup extra virgin olive oil
Salt to taste

Peel the plantains and slice on the bias into pieces that are about ½" thick. Set aside.

Place the oil in a small pan on a medium heat. Once the oil is hot, put the plantains in the pan and cook for 2 - 3 minutes on each side until golden brown.

Take off of the heat and blot off the excess oil.

Sprinkle lightly with salt.

Serve as a side dish.

The ENTIRETY of plantains fall under the PARENTAGE of the banana, but only a FINITE ALLOTMENT of bananas qualifies as plantains. There's one easy way to DIFFERENTIATE them: it's INADVISABLE to eat raw plantains because the PROPORTIONATE amount of starch contained makes them OPERATE more as a vegetable than a fruit. Thus, plantains are called, "the potato of the Caribbean," being enjoyed most when fried or baked. NOTICEABLE blackening of the skin, a sign of ripening, is MANDATORY if you insist on eating raw plantains.

———

ENTIRETY	limited
PARENTAGE	required
FINITE	discriminate
ALLOTMENT	act
DIFFERENTIATE	portion
INADVISABLE	corresponding
PROPORTIONATE	conspicuous
OPERATE	origin
NOTICEABLE	unwise
MANDATORY	whole

Roasted Butternut Squash With Dried Cranberries
Serves 4

1 medium butternut squash
5 tbsp dried cranberries
2 tbsp extra virgin olive oil
Salt and freshly ground black pepper to taste

Preheat the oven to 400° Fahrenheit.

Peel and halve the squash, scoop out the seeds and chop into 1" cubes.

Toss the squash, olive oil, and a pinch of salt and pepper on a large sheet pan. Roast, tossing occasionally with a spatula. Bake for about 20 minutes, and then add the cranberries.

Bake for another 10 - 15 minutes. The butternut squash is done when it becomes tender and slightly caramelized.

Serve.

As with butternut squash, humans can be roasted, but only in a FIGURATIVE sense. A roast is a function at which a REVERED individual is subject to JOVIAL BADGERING, CLOYING flattery and FLAMBOYANT praise. Speakers EXAGGERATE and tell OUTLANDISH, often RIBALD stories about the person. The GAIETY is designed to honor the roasted, insuring a good time will be had by all.

FIGURATIVE	vulgar
REVERE	pester
JOVIAL	zany
BADGER	admire
CLOYING	theatrical
FLAMBOYANT	festivity
EXAGGERATE	overly sweet
OUTLANDISH	friendly
RIBALD	symbolic
GAIETY	embellish

Rosemary And Thyme Scalloped Potatoes
Serves 4

2 pounds white potatoes
¾ cup frozen peas
¼ cup grated Swiss cheese
¼ cup grated Parmesan cheese
1¼ cups heavy cream
½ cup milk
1 sprig thyme
3 garlic cloves
1 sprig rosemary
¼ tsp cayenne pepper
Nonstick cooking spray
Salt and freshly ground black pepper to taste

Preheat the oven to 375° Fahrenheit.

Thinly slice the potatoes. Chop the garlic in half.

Prepare a small casserole dish by spraying it with nonstick cooking spray. On a low - medium heat, heat the heavy cream, milk, thyme, garlic, rosemary, and cayenne. Stir continuously until it reaches a gentle simmer. Remove the mixture from the heat, and discard the garlic, rosemary, and thyme. Add the frozen peas to the mixture and set aside.

In the casserole dish, lay the potatoes so they slightly overlap and cover the bottom of the dish. Place ¼ of the cream mixture and repeat this process 2 more times, ending with the cream. Bake for about 35 minutes, add the cheese and bake for another 10 - 15 minutes or until the cheese melts and starts to become golden.

Serve.

Scalloped potatoes are hearty but not HALE, a STIGMA this INDULGENCE can never escape. It's best to SUPPRESS all thoughts of calories, PROSCRIBE all talk of cholesterol at the dinner table, and make taste the only CRITERION needed to enjoy this VELVETY dish, which goes down easy. RECAPITULATE your pleasure the next day by reheating, because RETENTION of flavor and texture make scalloped potatoes ESTIMABLE leftovers.

HALE	appreciable
STIGMA	standard
INDULGENCE	flaw
SUPPRESS	holding
PROSCRIBE	luxury
CRITERION	repeat
VELVETY	healthy
RECAPITULATE	ban
RETENTION	restrain
ESTIMABLE	soft

Pork Buns
Makes about 15 medium buns

Pork:	Sauce:	Dough:
1⅓ lbs pork tenderloin	3 tbsp cornstarch	⅔ cup heavy cream
1½ tbsp low sodium soy sauce	3 tsp garlic powder	3 tbsp unsalted butter
1 tbsp white vinegar	¼ cup low sodium soy sauce	3 tbsp water
1 tbsp hoisin sauce	1 tbsp hoisin sauce	1 packet fast rising yeast
1 tbsp oyster sauce	1 tbsp honey	1 tsp honey + 2 tsp sugar
1 tbsp honey + extra to brush	¼ cup water	2 eggs
¼ tsp salt		1¾ cup flour + extra for kneading
¼ tsp pepper		1 tsp oil (any kind)

Preheat the oven to 450° Fahrenheit.

Chop the pork tenderloin into 3 pieces. Mix all of the pork ingredients in a large bowl. Place the pork on a medium tin foil-lined baking sheet. Bake it for 30 minutes, turning it every 10 minutes. Remove it from the oven and set aside. Reduce the oven to 350° Fahrenheit.

For the dough: heat the cream, butter, and water in a small saucepan until the mixture reaches 105° Fahrenheit, then set aside for a few minutes. Mix the yeast, honey and sugar in a large bowl and add the cream mixture, whisk it and set aside. In another bowl, combine the flour and 2 eggs and slowly stir this into the yeast. Whisk together (the dough will be very sticky). Sprinkle flour on a board and on your hands. Turn out the dough and lightly flour. Knead for 5 minutes. Keep adding sprinkles of flour so the dough doesn't stick. The end dough should be soft and elastic to the touch. Place in an oiled bowl and cover with a clean kitchen towel. Place in a warm area for about 1 hour.

Chop the pork into small chunks. Place it in a small saucepan with all of the sauce ingredients. Cook for about 5 minutes, stirring occasionally.

Once the dough has risen, punch it down and shape it into a 15" long log. Cut it into 15 sections and flatten each to a 4" diameter circle with your palm. Add 2 tsp of filling in the center of each dough circle. Bring up the edges and slightly twist to completely close the top. Place seam-side down on a large, nonstick baking sheet sprayed with cooking spray. Repeat this process for each bun. Bake for about 15 minutes. Lightly brush honey on each bun.

Serve.

"Cha siu baau," also RECOGNIZED as pork buns, an EXTRAORDINARY Cantonese specialty, are not a common American COMMODITY. The FORMULA for making the perfect pork bun involves roasting pork until it becomes "fall off the bone and CARTILAGE" tender, BASTING, cooking with fresh yeast so the dough can LEAVEN properly, and LADLING the right amount of pork onto the dough. The product ACCOMPLISHED by following these steps is sure to ENRAPTURE your guests.

RECOGNIZED	raise
EXTRAORDINARY	achieve
COMMODITY	remarkable
FORMULA	pouring juices
CARTILAGE	spooning
BASTING	product
LEAVEN	delight
LADLING	connective tissue
ACCOMPLISH	identified
ENRAPTURE	method

Vegetable Kabobs
Serves 5 (makes 10 kabobs)

2½ zucchini
1½ small red onions
1 medium bell pepper, any color
20 grape tomatoes
Extra virgin olive oil
Salt and freshly ground black pepper to taste

Soak 10 wooden kabob or skewer sticks in water for at least 30 minutes before baking to prevent complete charring.

Preheat the oven to 450° Fahrenheit.

Chop the zucchini into twenty ¼" slices. Chop the onions into twenty ¼" chunks. Chop the pepper into twenty chunks.

Place the vegetables on the skewer in any order. Each skewer should have 2 chunks of each vegetable. Place on a sheet pan and lightly drizzle with oil and sprinkle with salt and pepper. Bake for 20 - 25 minutes.

Serve.

Kebobs are grilled cubes of food aligned in SEQUENCE along a skewer. Their EXISTENCE is a tribute to human INTELLECT and the ability to be INVENTIVE. Persian soldiers used their swords, ANALOGOUS to today's skewer, to grill in the field. Battlefield conditions made supplies of cooking oil INADEQUATE, so only small amounts of food could be prepared at any time. APERTURES left between hot stones provided a SUFFICIENT amount of oxygen to stoke the fire. Cooking time was critical to achieve DISCERNIBLE charring but not INCINERATE the meal.

SEQUENCE	opening
EXISTENCE	lacking
INTELLECT	adequate
INVENTIVE	order
ANALOGOUS	destroy by burning
INADEQUATE	recognizable
APERTURE	comparable
SUFFICIENT	being
DISCERNIBLE	creative
INCINERATE	mind

Scallops Gratin
Serves 4

1½ lbs sea scallops
4 tbsp softened, unsalted butter
4 tbsp minced parsley
6 tbsp goat cheese
1 green onion
4 garlic cloves
4 tbsp lemon juice
1 tbsp Dijon mustard
8 tbsp panko breadcrumbs
4 tbsp extra virgin olive oil
4 tbsp broth, any type
Salt and freshly ground black pepper to taste

Preheat the oven to 400° Fahrenheit.

You can use either 4 small oven-safe pans or 1 large one.

Mince the onion and garlic.

Mix together the butter, parsley, goat cheese, green onion, garlic, lemon, Dijon mustard, panko, oil and a pinch of salt and pepper.

Place the broth in the bottom of the dish/dishes. Place the scallops in the pan and lightly salt. Add the butter mixture on top and bake for 10 - 12 minutes. You can broil it for another minute to create a crispier topping.

Serve.

The scallop shell is a FEMININE symbol that VISUALLY represents the PROTECTIVE and NURTURING PRINCIPLES of the SISTERHOOD. In PAGAN THEOLOGY it embodies both fertility and part of the SOLAR cycle, denoting the sun setting as the day TERMINATES. Its beautiful fan shape and bright colors add to the legend.

FEMININE	shielding
VISUAL	sun-related
PROTECTIVE	female association
NURTURE	woman-like
PRINCIPLE	religion
SISTERHOOD	idea
PAGAN	end
THEOLOGY	perceptible
SOLAR	non-Christian
TERMINATE	foster

Entrée

Margherita Panini (Tomato, Basil And Mozzarella Panini)
Fish In Parchment
Mushroom Risotto
Meat Lasagna
Cheese Cannelloni
Pesto Pizza
Tortellini With White Cream Sauce And Artichokes
Baked Macaroni
Rotini Primavera
Eggplant Parmesan
Ratatouille
Cheese Soufflé
Meal In A Pita Pocket
Lemon Shrimp With Garlic Sauce
Braised Short Ribs
Roasted Lemon Chicken With Pine Nut Couscous
Mediterranean Turkey Meatloaf
Fish Cakes
Fried Rice
Beef And Broccoli Stir-fry
Saffron Meatballs
Veggie Burger
Egg Salad
Poached Salmon With Dill Yogurt Sauce
Stuffed Peppers
Étouffée
Polish Stuffed Cabbage
Tofu Enchiladas
Ruby's Belizean Red Beans
Breakfast For Dinner (Buttermilk Biscuit With Poached Egg Florentine)
Vegetable Pot Pie
Turkey Tostada
Gourmet Grilled Cheese

Margherita Panini (Tomato, Basil And Mozzarella Panini)

Serves 1

1 Ciabatta loaf
4 slices mozzarella
4 slices tomato
4 basil leaves
2 tsp extra virgin olive oil
Salt and freshly ground black pepper to taste

Cut off an end of the Ciabatta loaf, then cut a 3" wide section from the end. Cut this in half to achieve 2 slices of bread, each about ½" thick. Place the mozzarella, tomato and basil on one slice of bread and sprinkle with salt and pepper. Place the other slice of bread on top. Drizzle 1 tsp of oil on the exterior of each bread slice.

To make a panini without a press, heat a grill pan and a sauté pan on a medium heat. Place the sandwich on the grill pan and the bottom of the sauté pan on the top of the sandwich. Remember to turn off the burner used with the sauté pan. Place a large cover on top of the pan and press down to create a panini.

Cook for 2 minutes, then flip and repeat.

Serve warm.

Tomatoes, mozzarella and basil are the TRIUMVIRATE of ingredients that VENERATE the Italian flag and RECOLLECT Margherita of Savoy, the GRANDILOQUENT Queen CONSORT of Italy, who inspired the combination. The original Margherita was a pizza but now ENCOMPASSES APPRECIABLY more VARIATION. COMPRESS a sandwich between two heated blades and you get a panini, in this case, one of notable PEERAGE.

TRIUMVIRATE	include
VENERATE	considerably
RECOLLECT	modification
GRANDILOQUENT	nobility
CONSORT	recall
ENCOMPASS	pompous
APPRECIABLY	flatten
VARIATION	companion
COMPRESS	threesome
PEERAGE	honor

Fish in Parchment
Serves 4

4 (6 oz) cleaned, deboned, skinned white fish, any type
7 oz shiitake mushrooms
4 asparagus stems
2 leek bottoms
3 large garlic cloves
2 tbsp honey
2 tbsp low sodium soy sauce
3 tbsp extra virgin olive oil
Salt and freshly ground black pepper to taste

Preheat the oven to 375° Fahrenheit.

Thinly slice the mushrooms, asparagus, leeks and garlic.

Place 4 (11" x 15") pieces of parchment paper in a row on a hard surface with 1 piece of fish at the center of each. Evenly distribute the mushrooms, asparagus, leeks and garlic on each piece of fish.

Whisk together the honey, soy sauce, oil, salt and pepper and pour ¼ of the mixture on each fish.

Carefully fold over and roll the top of the parchment and tuck each side under. Repeat this step for the remaining pouches. Line the pouches on a sheet pan and cook for 12 - 15 minutes.

Serve immediately.

Even if you are a TYRO trying to HONE your NASCENT skills, "in parchment" cooking will make you seem like a master chef. Guests will EXTOL your PROWESS, unaware of the deceptively simple preparation involved. It's LITERALLY a meal in a pouch, which makes the presentation unique. Offer each guest a plate upon which a TUMESCENT bag is perched. Demonstrate the art of carefully piercing the parchment, allowing the aroma to WAFT up and TITILLATE the OLFACTORY senses. Delight in the textures and flavors resulting from the steaming mixture. More than a meal, this dish guarantees an experience.

TYRO	float
HONE	objectively
NASCENT	swollen
EXTOL	stimulate
PROWESS	relating to smell
LITERALLY	skill
TUMESCENT	beginner
WAFT	praise
TITILLATE	sharpen
OLFACTORY	budding

Mushroom Risotto
Serves 4

1 cup white Arborio rice
2 large Portobello mushrooms
1 small white onion
5 cups broth
3 tbsp unsalted butter
1 tbsp extra virgin olive oil
½ cup grated Parmesan cheese
Salt and freshly ground black pepper to taste

Clean the mushrooms with a damp paper towel and dice into bite size chunks. Chop the onion into small chunks.

In a small pot, heat the broth to a gentle simmer and keep it warm on a low heat.

Meanwhile, heat the butter and oil in a large, heavy pot. Add the mushrooms and onion to the pot and cook on a medium - high heat for about 5 minutes, stirring occasionally. Reduce the heat to low and add the rice, stirring constantly for 1 minute. Add a pinch of salt and pepper. Keep the heat on low and add ½ cup of warm stock to the rice and stir continuously until it is almost completely absorbed. Keep adding broth, ½ cup at a time until you have used all of the stock. The finished rice should be gooey and slightly coated from the thickened sauce.

Mix in the Parmesan cheese and serve immediately.

You might GUESS that while NIMBLE chefs are NONCHALANT about cooking risotto, not all of us are as PERSPICACIOUS. The recipe is guaranteed to VEX the average student of culinary arts because it is NOTORIOUSLY difficult to master. Carry on! You might appear HAGGARD, but the GUSTO your guests show when you serve the meal will be an INVALUABLE PERQUISITE of your effort.

GUESS	enjoyment
NIMBLE	precious
NONCHALANT	infamous
PERSPICACIOUS	benefit
VEX	surmise
NOTORIOUS	astute
HAGGARD	quick
GUSTO	worn
INVALUABLE	indifferent
PERQUISITE	irritate

Meat Lasagna
Serves 10 - 12

1 lb ground beef
½ pound sausage, any kind
1 small - medium white onion
2 tbsp fresh minced parsley
4 garlic cloves
1 (8 oz) can plain tomato sauce

1 (28 oz) jar marinara sauce, any kind
1 (16 oz) package lasagna noodles
1 (15 oz) container whole milk ricotta cheese
2 eggs, beaten
¼ cup milk

16 oz mozzarella cheese, shredded
¼ cup grated Parmesan cheese
2 tbsp minced fresh basil
1 tbsp extra virgin olive oil
Salt and freshly ground black pepper to taste

Preheat the oven to 375° Fahrenheit.

Mince the onion and garlic cloves.

Heat the oil in a medium pot on a medium - high heat. Brown the beef, sausage, onion, and a pinch of salt and pepper. Stir with a wooden spoon to break the meat and sausage into small pieces. Cook for about 6 minutes. Add the parsley and garlic, and cook for another 2 minutes or until the meats are completely brown. Drain the mixture in a strainer, and set aside.

In a large pot, heat up the tomato and marinara sauces on a medium heat. Add the meat and vegetable mixture and cook for about 20 minutes. Remove from the heat and set aside.

In a bowl, combine the ricotta, milk, eggs, and a pinch of salt and pepper.

Cook the lasagna noodles according to the manufacturer's instructions. To assemble the lasagna, cover the bottom of a 9" x 13" baking dish with meat sauce. Cover the bottom of the baking dish with lasagna noodles, then cover with more sauce and spread with ⅓ of the ricotta mixture and then top with ⅓ of the mozzarella cheese. Repeat this process 2 more times, ending with the ricotta cheese mixture, mozzarella cheese, and Parmesan. Cover the dish with tin foil and bake covered for about 30 minutes. Uncover and the bake for another 15 minutes. Let cool at least 15 minutes before serving.

Sprinkle the fresh basil on top and serve.

Garfield is the FICTITIOUS comic strip cat who is not ABSTEMIOUS when it comes to lasagna, the flat, OBLONG pasta that is his obsession. The TELLTALE sign of this passion is his OBESITY and DISTENSIBLE stomach, which he displays with FLAGRANT indifference. His LEONINE personality and OBSTREPEROUS behavior have not WANED through time.

FICTITIOUS	lion-like
ABSTEMIOUS	boisterous
OBLONG	giveaway
TELLTALE	elongated
OBESITY	restrained
DISTENSIBLE	fabricated
FLAGRANT	decrease
LEONINE	being grossly overweight
OBSTREPEROUS	stretchable
WANE	conspicuous

Cheese Cannelloni
Serves 6

12 lasagna sheets (will be rolled into "cannelloni")
1 medium white onion
½ cup spinach
¼ cup arugula
2 garlic cloves
1 tbsp unsalted butter
1 tbsp extra virgin olive oil
4 cups ricotta cheese
1 cup grated Parmesan cheese
1 cup grated mozzarella cheese
24 oz jarred marinara sauce + more to taste
Salt and freshly ground black pepper to taste

Preheat the oven to 375° Fahrenheit.

You will need a 13" x 9" baking dish.

Mince the onion and garlic cloves.

Cook the lasagna according to the manufacturer's directions.

Heat the oil and butter in a medium pan on a medium heat. Cook the onion and garlic for about 3 minutes. Add the spinach and arugula and cook for another 2 minutes.

In a large bowl, mix together the ricotta cheese, Parmesan, mozzarella and cooked vegetable mixture. Salt and pepper to taste.

Place the lasagna on a board and fill it with ⅓ cup of the mixture. Roll it up and complete the rest of the sheets.

Place 1 cup of the sauce on the bottom of the baking dish. Place the cannelloni rolls seam side down in the sauce. Place the remaining sauce on top and bake for about 35 minutes.

Serve.

Cannelloni, often ERRONEOUSLY confused with manicotti, is large, tubular pasta. Take the "milky" out of MILKY WAY and select the best CREAMY cheese you can find for the filling. Chefs whose FORTÉ is cannelloni can enter a holiday cooking contest in Catalonia, Italy each December. They DECORATE the dish with a variety of toppings in effort to OUTDO the competition. It's part of a weeklong celebration during which couples are BETROTHED, attend a MINISTRY, and OSCULATE in BLISS.

ERRONEOUS	adorn
MILKY WAY	buttery
CREAMY	kiss
FORTÉ	prayer
DECORATE	galaxy
OUTDO	incorrect
BETROTHED	beat
MINISTRY	ecstasy
OSCULATE	engaged
BLISS	talent

Pesto Pizza
Serves 5

2 cups fresh packed basil leaves + 10 leaves
¼ cup nuts (walnuts, pine nuts, or a combination)
4 garlic cloves
½ cup extra virgin olive oil
½ cup Parmesan cheese
1 (1 lb) store bought pizza dough
8 oz mozzarella cheese
1 medium vine tomato
1 tbsp corn meal
Flour for rolling out the dough
Salt and freshly ground pepper to taste

Preheat the oven to 450° Fahrenheit.

Thinly slice the mozzarella cheese and vine tomato.

In a food processor or blender, pulse the 2 cups of basil, nuts, and garlic until minced. Slowly pour in the olive oil through the feed tube. Transfer the mixture to a bowl and stir in the Parmesan cheese. Set aside.

Flour a clean surface and your hands. Roll and stretch the pizza dough until it is very thin.

Sprinkle the corn meal on a baking sheet and gently place the dough on top. Bake for about 3 minutes. Remove from the oven. Top with the pesto, tomato slices, extra basil, and mozzarella, making sure to leave a 1" border.

Place in the oven and cook for 8 - 10 minutes or until the pizza is golden and cooked.

Slice and serve.

Pine Nut Syndrome, a TRANSIENT disturbance causing food to taste ACERBIC and metallic, is a random occurrence according to one HYPOTHESIS. A more SINISTER view IMPLICATES the use of tainted COUNTERFEIT nuts, which, while INEDIBLE, have been sold as the real thing. The UTMOST caution should be used in avoiding the use of SPURIOUS ingredients. High quality will never SUBVERT a meal, or your health.

TRANSIENT	phony
ACERBIC	involve
HYPOTHESIS	bitter
SINISTER	fake
IMPLICATE	uneatable
COUNTERFEIT	greatest
INEDIBLE	undermine
UTMOST	evil
SPURIOUS	impermanent
SUBVERT	theory

Tortellini with White Cream Sauce and Artichokes
Serves 4

12 oz store bought cheese tortellini
9 oz artichoke hearts (if frozen/canned, make sure to thaw/drain before use)
2 garlic cloves
¼ cup mascarpone cheese, room temperature
1 tbsp flour
1 cup milk
1 tbsp extra virgin olive oil
Salt and freshly ground black pepper to taste

Cook the tortellini according to the manufacturer's instructions.

Mince the garlic cloves.

Add the artichokes, olive oil, garlic, and a pinch of salt and pepper to a large pot on a medium heat. Cook, stirring occasionally for about 3 minutes.

Add the mascarpone, milk and flour, and cook on a high heat until the mixture just starts to bubble. Reduce the heat to low, and cook, stirring occasionally for about 3 minutes.

Toss with the pasta.

Serve.

No APOLOGY needed if you are ANXIOUS that how to cook and eat artichokes seems so ARBITRARY. The topic is DEBATABLE and clearly, it takes more than INTUITION to become skilled at something that doesn't come NATURALLY. The task is VINCIBLE so have the FORTITUDE to persist, and don't FORGO including this tasty ALIMENT in your meal plans.

APOLOGY	unpredictable
ANXIOUS	conquerable
ARBITRARY	intuitiveness
DEBATABLE	explanation
INTUITION	food
NATURALLY	sacrifice
VINCIBLE	bravery
FORTITUDE	disputable
FORGO	innately
ALIMENT	concerned

Baked Macaroni
Serves 8 - 10

1 lb elbow macaroni
2 cups grated white cheddar cheese
2 cups grated sharp cheddar cheese
1 vine tomato
4½ cups milk
3 tbsp unsalted butter
3 tbsp flour
1 tsp salt + more to taste
½ tsp pepper + more to taste
¼ tsp cayenne pepper + more to taste
1 cup panko breadcrumbs
3 tbsp oil, any type

Preheat the oven to 375° Fahrenheit.

Cook the macaroni according to the manufacturer's directions. Slice the tomato into ¼"
rounds.

For the sauce: melt the butter on a medium heat in a large pot, and then stir in the flour, salt,
pepper, and cayenne. Cook for about 2 minutes, stirring constantly. Slowly pour in the milk
and bring to a slight simmer. Reduce the heat to low and cook, stirring occasionally until
the sauce thickens (about 10 minutes). Add both cheeses and remove from the heat. Stir until
everything melts together. Taste the sauce for seasoning.

Add the macaroni and stir. Transfer the mixture to a large baking dish. Top with the tomatoes.

In a separate bowl, mix together the panko and oil and spoon over the tomatoes. Bake for
about 45 minutes - 1 hour, or until the panko is golden brown.

Allow the baked macaroni to cool for at least 10 minutes before serving.

There's nothing PRETENTIOUS about a meal that can be bought by PATRONIZING the local CONVENIENCE store, so it may be a surprise that mac and cheese was a favorite of Italian PATRICIANS until the 18th century. This dish was known to SATIATE the appetite of President Jefferson, a FERVENT fan who served it at the White House on at least one FESTIVE occasion. Cooking macaroni with two cheeses may be SLIGHTLY OSTENTATIOUS, but it tastes great and maintains FIDELITY to the original concept.

PRETENTIOUS	aristocrat
PATRONIZING	flashy
CONVENIENCE	faithfulness
PATRICIAN	celebratory
SATIATE	frequenting
FERVENT	snobbish
FESTIVE	somewhat
SLIGHTLY	enthusiastic
OSTENTATIOUS	accessibility
FIDELITY	satisfy

Rotini Primavera
Serves 4

8 ounces rotini pasta
2 medium zucchini
1 medium red onion
20 – 25 grape tomatoes
⅓ cup tomato sauce
2 tbsp unsalted butter
1 tbsp oil
Salt and freshly ground black pepper to taste

For the vegetable sauce: chop the zucchini and onion into about ¼" chunks. Place the butter, oil, zucchini and onion on a medium heat. Allow to cook for about 8 minutes or until the vegetables are soft and golden, stirring occasionally.

Meanwhile, slice the grape tomatoes in half. Add the tomatoes and a sprinkle of salt and pepper to the pot. Reduce the heat to low and stir occasionally for 3 minutes. Next, add the tomato sauce and cook for 3 minutes. Remove from the heat.

*Tip: For added flavor, add 1 tsp of chipotle pepper flakes.

For the rotini: fill a medium size pot with water and bring to a rapid boil. Add a sprinkle of salt to the water, add pasta and follow the cooking time on the box.

Once the rotini is cooked, toss it with the vegetable sauce.

Serve immediately.

Pasta meals should never be MONOTONOUS because there are INFINITE varieties available. An ENCYCLOPEDIA of shapes would include LINEAR fettuccine, CONVEX capunti, CYCLOID wagon wheels, SPHEROID pastina and wide CIRCUMFERENCE manicotti. Rotini has a corkscrew shape, which makes it appear to GYRATE. The CORPOREAL characteristics of pasta also include different sizes and colors, giving chefs many decisions to make.

MONOTONOUS	comprehensive book
INFINITE	curving as the surface of a circle
ENCYCLOPEDIA	like a circle
LINEAR	rotate
CONVEX	perimeter
CYCLOID	bodily
SPHEROID	dull
CIRCUMFERENCE	straight
GYRATE	sphere-like
CORPOREAL	limitless

Eggplant Parmesan
Serves 8

3 medium eggplants (3 lbs)
2 cups tomato sauce
2¼ cups shredded mozzarella cheese
2 cups grated Parmesan cheese
Salt and freshly ground black pepper to taste

Preheat the oven to 350° Fahrenheit.

Hold the eggplant upright and cut it into ½" thick lengthwise slices. Place the slices on a 12" x 9" baking pan and bake for about 45 minutes. Remove the eggplant from the pan and spread ½ cup of tomato sauce on the bottom.

Layer ⅓ of the eggplant on the bottom, then top it with ½ cup tomato sauce, ½ cup each of both cheeses and sprinkle with salt and pepper. Repeat this process for the second layer of eggplant.

For the top, add another layer of eggplant and spread ½ cup tomato sauce on it. Sprinkle with salt and pepper. Finish with 1 cup Parmesan cheese and 1¼ cups mozzarella.

Bake for 40 minutes or until lightly golden and let sit for 10 minutes before serving.

Eggplant Parmesan is VEGETARIAN SUSTENANCE that can easily be modified to ACCOMMODATE your CARNIVOROUS guests by AUGMENTING the recipe with ground beef. Cook a generous QUANTITY that can be stored for a PROTRACTED length of time, enough for many EVENTUAL meals. Preparation of the dish is time INTENSIVE but reheated eggplant Parmesan remains as IRRESISTIBLE as it was on the day it was made.

VEGETARIAN	meat lover
SUSTENANCE	tempting
ACCOMMODATE	prolong
CARNIVOROUS	amount
AUGMENT	exhaustive
QUANTITY	meatless
PROTRACT	increase
EVENTUAL	help
INTENSIVE	food
IRRESISTIBLE	ultimate

Ratatouille
Serves 4

1 medium eggplant
1 medium white onion
1 small zucchini
2 large tomatoes
1 small yellow squash
1 medium red bell pepper
2 garlic cloves
½ cup tomato sauce
¼ cup chicken broth
1 tbsp fresh chopped parsley
1 tbsp fresh minced thyme
1 bay leaf
4 tbsp extra virgin olive oil
Salt and freshly ground black pepper to taste
Red pepper flakes (optional)

Chop the eggplant, onion, zucchini, tomatoes, yellow squash and bell pepper into 1" chunks. Sliver the garlic.

Heat the oil on a medium heat in a large pot. Add the onions, and cook, stirring occasionally, for about 6 minutes. Add the garlic and cook for another minute. Add the rest of the ingredients, reduce the heat to low, cover, and cook for about 1 hour or until the vegetables are tender.

Serve.

*Tip: Add a sprinkle of red pepper flakes to make the dish spicy.

"Ratatouille" can be considered a HOMONYM since it refers to a vegetable stew as well as an academy award-winning movie about a QUIXOTIC rodent with a PENCHANT for cooking. In the movie, ratatouille served to a FASTIDIOUS restaurant critic saves the day by unleashing a REPOSITORY of childhood memories. The experience ANIMATES his enthusiasm, and the critic REVISES a previously DETRIMENTAL review. The DUTIFUL and PRODUCTIVE rodent achieves his dream and, as expected, everyone lives happily ever after.

HOMONYM	idealistic
QUIXOTIC	injurious
PENCHANT	same sound/different meaning
FASTIDIOUS	devoted
REPOSITORY	prolific
ANIMATE	modify
REVISE	enliven
DETRIMENTAL	meticulous
DUTIFUL	storage place
PRODUCTIVE	liking

Cheese Soufflé
Serves 2

2 tbsp grated Parmesan cheese
½ cup grated Gruyere cheese
3 tbsp goat cheese
3 tbsp unsalted butter
2¼ tsp flour
½ cup milk
2 eggs, yolk and white separated
⅛ tsp nutmeg
Salt and freshly ground black pepper to taste

Preheat the oven to 375° Fahrenheit.

Grease two 8 oz ramekins with 1 tbsp butter. Place ½ of the Parmesan in each ramekin and tap it around so it sticks to the sides. Discard the extra Parmesan, if there is any left.

To make the soufflé, melt 2 tbsp butter on a medium heat. Add the flour and cook for about 1 minute. Stir in the nutmeg, and a pinch of salt and pepper. Add the milk and cook for about 1½ minutes or until it starts to boil. Make sure to stir. Add the cheeses and the egg yolks, and stir until everything is completely incorporated. Set aside and allow the mixture to cool.

In another bowl, whip the egg whites until they form stiff peaks. It is best to use an electric mixer for this step. Gently fold the whites into the cooled cheese mixture. Evenly spoon this mixture into the ramekins and bake for about 20 minutes.

Serve immediately.

The ability to beat eggs perfectly is the challenge a chef must SURMOUNT to make soufflé. It is IMPERATIVE to SUBTRAHEND every last bit of yolk from the egg whites to SAFEGUARD the ability of the TRANSLUCENT gel to AGGLOMERATE air and rise. Anything less than complete separation will UNDERMINE the effort and IMPERIL the outcome. PERSEVERANCE is the key to PROFICIENCY.

SURMOUNT	subtract
IMPERATIVE	semitransparent
SUBTRAHEND	overcome
SAFEGUARD	jeopardize
TRANSLUCENT	necessary
AGGLOMERATE	weaken
UNDERMINE	aggregate
IMPERIL	protect
PERSEVERANCE	skill
PROFICIENCY	dedication

Meal In A Pita Pocket
Serves 1 - 2

1 pita pocket, sliced in half
4 button mushrooms
½ red onion
1 small tomato
½ cup baby spinach
1 small avocado
1 small lemon, juiced
1 tbsp minced jalapeño pepper
3 tbsp plain hummus
½ small cucumber
3 tbsp Greek yogurt
1 tbsp extra virgin olive oil
Salt and freshly ground black pepper to taste

Thinly slice the mushrooms, onion and tomato, and separate the onion into rings. Peel and dice the cucumber. Mash the avocado.

Sauté the mushrooms, onion, and a pinch of salt and pepper in the oil on a medium - high heat. Cook, stirring occasionally for about 5 minutes. Add the spinach and cook until it wilts, another 1 - 2 minutes. Salt and pepper to taste. Set aside.

Combine the avocado, lemon juice, and jalapeño in a bowl and mix until it resembles a sauce. Set aside.

Combine the yogurt and cucumber in a bowl, and set aside.

Place the pita halves in a pan on a medium - high heat and cook on each side for about 1 - 2 minutes.

To assemble the pockets, place half of each vegetable and half of each sauce (the hummus, avocado, and yogurt) into each half pocket.

Serve.

*Tip: Add grilled chicken and/or crumbled feta cheese for extra flavor.

It is PLAUSIBLE that the discovery of pita, a flatbread pocket, might have been an INSTANCE of SHEER luck. Some PROMULGATE the theory that an OBSERVANT individual noted the INFLUX of steam during baking served to puff up and EXPAND the dough, forming a pocket when the bread cooled and flattened. One thing is for sure: the popularity of pita continues to be EXPLOSIVE. A good PRECAUTION is to avoid excessive ARDOR in making this meal: overstuffing the pocket can land some of it in your lap!

PLAUSIBLE	increasing
INSTANCE	possible
SHEER	watchful
PROMULGATE	safeguard
OBSERVANT	utter
INFLUX	enthusiasm
EXPAND	flow
EXPLOSIVE	proclaim
PRECAUTION	case
ARDOR	enlarge

Lemon Shrimp With Garlic Sauce
Serves 2 - 3

Shrimp:
1 lb cleaned shrimp
½ tsp salt
½ tsp pepper
1 tbsp extra virgin olive oil

Garlic Sauce:
4 garlic cloves
3½ tbsp unsalted butter
¼ tsp salt
¼ tsp pepper
1 lemon, juice and zest

For the garlic sauce: mince the garlic cloves. Melt the butter with the salt, pepper, garlic, and the juice and zest of a lemon on a low heat. Once completely melted, stir and take the mixture off of the heat and allow it to sit for about 10 minutes.

For the shrimp: season with the salt, pepper, and oil. Heat a grill pan on high. Once hot, place the shrimp on the pan and cook for about 2 - 3 minutes on each side until bright pink in color.

Serve with the sauce.

Making CLARIFIED butter is a FACILE task that doesn't require MEDITATION when taken step by step. PURL any amount of cream in a food processor or stand mixer until it resembles butter, at which point it's READY to be drained. To achieve a CESSATION in the PROGRESSION to BITTERNESS caused by aging, process the butter with ice water and repeat until the EXTRANEOUS liquid is no longer OPAQUE.

CLARIFIED	superfluous
FACILE	cloudy
MEDITATION	movement
PURL	easy
READY	clear
CESSATION	harshness
PROGRESSION	stir
BITTERNESS	prepared
EXTRANEOUS	end
OPAQUE	contemplation

Braised Short Ribs
Serves 2

2 whole short ribs, about 1½ lbs each and 7" in length
2 carrots
1 zucchini
2 celery stalks
1 small white onion
1 medium Idaho potato
1 (8 oz) can tomato sauce
1 (14.5 oz) can stewed tomatoes
1 cup broth (chicken, beef, or vegetable)
2 tbsp unsalted butter
2 tsp dried thyme
2 tsp ground rosemary
1 tbsp extra virgin olive oil
Salt and freshly ground black pepper to taste

Peel the carrots. Quarter the carrots and zucchini lengthwise. Chop the carrots, zucchini, celery and onion into 1" chunks. Peel the potato, quarter lengthwise and chop into ½" chunks.

Melt the butter and oil in a large Dutch oven on a high heat. Generously salt and pepper each side of the short ribs. Place in the pot and cook on each side for about 2 minutes. Remove from the pot and set aside.

Place all of the vegetables in the pot and let cook, stirring occasionally in the same fat that cooked the meat, for about 5 minutes. Sprinkle lightly with salt and pepper and add the herbs. Place the meat back into the pot, add the tomato sauce, stewed tomatoes, and the broth. Cover and cook on low just so the liquid gently simmers, for about 2½ hours. Spoon off any of the extra fat that renders from the meat.

Serve the beef, vegetables, and sauce over pasta, rice, or couscous.

In cooking, the TRANSITION from tough to tender can be accomplished by braising, a technique that works well for meat, poultry and vegetables. First, SEAR the meat, then cover with liquid and simmer, bake, or, to be AVANT-GARDE, barbecue. Broth, water, wine or a combination, are the common liquids used to coax and INFUSE flavor into the meat and sauce. FRUGAL chefs can create SUMPTUOUS meals from INEXPENSIVE cuts of meat. Preparation time is VARIABLE and CONTINGENT upon your choice of main ingredient. Braising allows the most PUSILLANIMOUS chef to experience success in the kitchen.

TRANSITION	conditional
SEAR	timid
AVANT-GARDE	rich
INFUSE	economical
FRUGAL	changing
SUMPTUOUS	cutting edge
INEXPENSIVE	passage
VARIABLE	introduce
CONTINGENT	char
PUSILLANIMOUS	low-priced

Roasted Lemon Chicken With Pine Nut Couscous
Serves 4

Chicken:
4 chicken breasts
¼ tsp thyme
7 garlic cloves
¼ tsp ground rosemary
8 slices, thinly sliced lemon
Zest of one lemon
Salt and freshly ground black pepper to taste

Couscous:
1 (6 oz) package instant couscous
½ cup pine nuts
8 garlic cloves
1 tsp pepper
¼ cup extra virgin olive oil

Preheat the oven to 375° Fahrenheit.

Mince the garlic.

For the chicken: drizzle the bottom of a small baking dish with oil. Place the chicken in the baking dish. Add all of the seasonings and mix well. Place 2 slices of lemon on each chicken breast, cover with tin foil and refrigerate for 1½ hours. Remove the tin foil and place the chicken, including the slices of lemon, in the oven for about 40 minutes.

For the couscous: follow the manufacturer's instructions for preparation. Place the nuts, garlic, oil, and pepper in a food processor or blender and process so the mixture resembles a paste. Scrape the sides as needed. Mix together the couscous and pine nut mixture.

Serve a scoop of couscous with each chicken breast.

Making couscous can be quite the TRAVAIL, because it's PHENOMENALLY ABSORBING. Semolina is mixed with water, flour, and salt and PROGRESSIVELY worked into smaller and ever more DIMINUTIVE pieces, and then steamed. It's your PREROGATIVE to choose the more EXPEDIENT solution, the store bought variety. Modern machinery ABBREVIATES the process of crushing couscous and DOMINATES the market. Couscous symbolizes luck, PROSPERITY, and many blessings, so eat up!

TRAVAIL	shorten
PHENOMENAL	gradually
ABSORBING	exceptional
PROGRESSIVELY	tiny
DIMINUTIVE	consuming
PREROGATIVE	rule
EXPEDIENT	struggle
ABBREVIATE	right
DOMINATE	wealth
PROSPERITY	hasty

Mediterranean Turkey Meatloaf
Serves 5 - 6

1⅓ lbs lean ground turkey
1 (7 oz) can sun-dried tomatoes
⅓ cup crumbled feta cheese
1 cup baby arugula
1 small white onion
1 tsp pepper
2 eggs
¼ tsp salt
1 tbsp flour
1 tsp garlic powder
Extra virgin olive oil

Preheat the oven to 350° Fahrenheit.

Chop the onion.

Drain the oil from the sun-dried tomatoes and chop them into thin strips.

Mix together all of the ingredients except for the olive oil.

Oil a 9" x 5" loaf pan and place the meatloaf mixture into the pan. Smooth the top for an even layer.

Bake for about 50 minutes and let sit for 10 minutes before serving.

Allow tomatoes to BASK in the RADIANCE of the warm Mediterranean sun and they will DEHYDRATE, a NECESSARY condition for the production of sun-dried tomatoes. The sun causes PERCEPTIBLE SHRINKAGE, as much as 90%, as the tomatoes SHRIVEL. The process does not DEPLETE the tomatoes of their nutrients, which is a BENEFIT. Sun-dried tomatoes add a little VITALITY to the turkey loaf.

BASK	dry out
RADIANCE	advantage
DEHYDRATE	recognizable
NECESSARY	lessen
PERCEPTIBLE	sparkle
SHRINKAGE	wrinkle
SHRIVEL	lounge
DEPLETE	zest
BENEFIT	contraction
VITALITY	indispensable

Fish Cakes
Makes 8 fish patties

1½ lbs cleaned, deboned, skinned cod fillets
¾ cup whole milk
3 slices white bread
1 small green bell pepper
¼ cup minced arugula
1 small white onion
1 lime, juiced
⅓ cup mayonnaise
1 tsp minced jalapeño pepper (+ more for extra spicy fish cakes)
3½ tbsp extra virgin olive oil
Salt and freshly ground black pepper to taste
Nonstick cooking spray

Preheat the oven to 375° Fahrenheit.

Spray a baking dish with nonstick cooking spray and place an even layer of cod fillets on the bottom. Pour the milk over the fish and bake for 30 – 35 minutes. Drain the milk and flake the fish with a fork.

Mince the bell pepper and onion. Mince the white bread or process into fine crumbs in a food processor.

Warm a skillet to a medium heat. Add ⅓ of the breadcrumbs and cook for a few minutes or until they are golden. Place them in a bowl. Add the fish, bell pepper, arugula, onion, lime juice, mayonnaise, jalapeño and a pinch of salt and pepper. Mix together.

Heat the oil in a large skillet on a medium heat.

While the oil is heating, form the fish batter into about 8 patties. Roll them in the remaining breadcrumbs. Place them in the skillet and cook for about 5 - 6 minutes per side or until golden brown.

Serve immediately.

A quick GLIMPSE at the TOPOGRAPHY of an area is a DECISIVE way to find the typical cuisine of a region. For fish cakes, any DOMAIN INHOSPITABLE to sea life could be PREDICTABLY DISCARDED. HABITANTS would likely live ADJACENT to bodies of water, including ESTUARIES. Luckily, you don't have to live seaside to enjoy this hearty meal.

GLIMPSE	can be foretold
TOPOGRAPHY	denizen
DECISIVE	adjoining
DOMAIN	narrow body of water
INHOSPITABLE	reject
PREDICTABLY	unwelcoming
DISCARD	look
HABITANT	area
ADJACENT	definite
ESTUARY	physical feature

Fried Rice
Serves 4 - 5

Rice:
4 cups chicken broth or water
2 cups white rice
2 tbsp oil or unsalted butter
Pinch of salt
Salt and freshly ground black pepper to taste

Vegetables:
½ cup diced baby carrots
½ cup frozen peas
2 eggs, beaten
¼ cup chopped scallions, white and green
4 tbsp low sodium soy sauce
1 tbsp oyster sauce
3 tbsp extra virgin olive oil

For the rice: combine all of the ingredients in a medium pot on a high heat and cover. Cook until the liquid is boiling, then reduce the heat to low and cook for about 15 minutes or until the water has fully absorbed and the rice is cooked. Set aside.

For the vegetables: cover the carrots with water and cook on a high heat for 5 minutes. Add the peas and cook for another 2 minutes. Drain and set aside.

Heat the oil in a large pot on a medium heat, and scramble the eggs for about 1 - 2 minutes. Using the back of a wooden spoon, break up the eggs into small pieces. Mix in the rice, peas, carrots, scallions, soy sauce and oyster sauce. Cook for about 1 minute until everything is well combined.

Serve.

Fried rice is typically cooked with a MISCELLANY of leftovers. The sight of veggies, meat and eggs all fried together is an OCULAR SENSATION and its taste won't disappoint. It's easy to TAILOR it to your LIKING by CULLING favorite spices and seasonings, and adding them to the mix. For those in a hurry, fried rice is sold at fast-food restaurants, those that offer EFFICIENT but IMPERSONAL SERVICE. It is often the PENULTIMATE dish at Chinese banquets, served immediately before dessert.

MISCELLANY	select
OCULAR	next to last
SENSATION	preference
TAILOR	inattentive
LIKING	fit
CULL	organized
EFFICIENT	assistance
IMPERSONAL	visual
SERVICE	knockout
PENULTIMATE	mixture

Beef And Broccoli Stir-fry
Serves 4

2 cups cubed stewing beef (chuck)
1¼ cups of water
1 lb broccoli florets
1 small white onion
½ cup low sodium soy sauce
⅛ cup oyster sauce
⅛ cup ketchup
2 tsp garlic powder
1½ tsp minced garlic
½ tsp salt
1 tsp pepper
3 tbsp extra virgin olive oil

Slice the beef into 2" strips and dice the onion.

Mix the beef, ¼ cup water, ¼ cup soy sauce, oyster sauce, ketchup, salt, pepper, garlic powder, and minced garlic. Set aside.

In a large pot, add 1 cup of water and the broccoli. Cover and cook on a high heat for about 5 minutes or until bright green in color. Remove from the heat and drain the water.

In a large saucepan on a medium heat, add the oil and the beef with the sauce and onion. Sauté, stirring occasionally, for 6 minutes. Add the broccoli and the other ¼ cup soy sauce and cook for another 4 minutes.

Serve over rice.

It's a VALID concern that the word "umami" might be FOREIGN to your ears. It is the fifth taste bud, which OUGHT to receive more appreciation. Japan, known for KIMONOS, its classic APPAREL, is also recognized because its foods are RIFE with umami, a pleasing, savory taste. Umami may not be TOLERABLE in ISOLATION, but when combined with other ingredients...the music of CELESTIAL beings will be heard OUTRIGHT!

VALID	full
FOREIGN	Japanese robe
OUGHT	alone
KIMONO	well-founded
APPAREL	heavenly
RIFE	should
TOLERABLE	completely
ISOLATION	unfamiliar
CELESTIAL	clothes
OUTRIGHT	bearable

Saffron Meatballs
Makes about 15 meatballs

Meatballs:
32 oz ground beef
½ tsp paprika
1 tsp garlic powder
1 pinch saffron, crumbled between your fingers (¼ tsp)
1 medium shallot
4 garlic cloves
2 eggs, beaten
1 tsp salt
1 tsp pepper
5 tbsp extra virgin olive oil
1 tbsp flour + 3 tbsp extra for rolling

Sauce:
3 cups broth (chicken, beef, veal or vegetable)
1 tbsp tomato paste
1 pinch saffron
¼ tsp chipotle pepper flakes

Mince the shallot and garlic.

For the meatballs: combine all of the ingredients in a medium bowl. Shape the meat into 2" rounds. Place the 3 tbsp of rolling flour on a plate and roll each meatball lightly to dust. Set aside.

Heat the oil in a nonstick pan on a medium heat. Add the meatballs and cook on each side for about 3 - 4 minutes or until golden brown. Add all of the sauce ingredients. Stir, cover, and reduce the heat to low.

Cook the meatballs for about 25 minutes and serve with a little of the broth over your favorite pasta. Salt to taste.

Serve.

*Tip: Serve saffron meatballs on their own as an appetizer.

Saffron has the REDOUBTABLE reputation for being the world's most expensive spice. It is FORTUITOUS that only a MEAGER amount can add enough flavor and color to satisfy even the most PARSIMONIOUS chef. Wooden cooking IMPLEMENTS absorb the saffron and should be avoided. Beyond price, JUDICIOUS use of these DIAPHANOUS threads PRECLUDES the ACRID taste, PUNGENT odor and medicinal quality that can result from too much of an otherwise good thing.

REDOUBTABLE	bitter
FORTUITOUS	delicate
MEAGER	sharp
PARSIMONIOUS	tool
IMPLEMENT	prevent
JUDICIOUS	lucky
DIAPHANOUS	stingy
PRECLUDE	sensible
ACRID	small
PUNGENT	formidable

Veggie Burger
Serves 4

1 (15 oz) can chickpeas
1 small red bell pepper
1 small red onion
3 tbsp cooked corn kernels
1 egg
1 tsp cumin
3 garlic cloves
2 tbsp rolled oats
1 tsp chili powder
½ cup breadcrumbs
1 tbsp minced parsley
2 tbsp extra virgin olive oil
Salt and freshly ground pepper to taste

Drain, rinse and dry the chickpeas. Dice the bell pepper and onion. Mince the garlic.

Place all of the ingredients, except for the oil, in a medium bowl. Use clean hands to mix everything together. Once the chickpeas are mashed and everything is combined, (you will know when the mixture is the right consistency, if, when pressed together, it resembles ground beef by holding its shape) divide the mixture into four patties. Shape them and then wrap them in plastic wrap and refrigerate them for about 45 minutes.

Once you are ready to cook the patties, heat the oil in a skillet on a medium heat. Cook the burgers on each side for about 2 - 3 minutes.

Serve on a bun with your favorite vegetables and condiments.

The average vegetarian expresses ABHORRENCE at the thought of eating ENTRAILS. Such HERBIVOROUS individuals RUE any harm done to animals. HENPECKED chefs who wish to avoid having their reputations RAVAGED by the HEINOUS crime of serving meat don't have to QUIBBLE. APPEASE the anger and induce a PASSIVE state by putting veggie burgers on the menu.

ABHORRENCE	sinful
ENTRAILS	allay
HERBIVOROUS	disgust
RUE	destroy
HENPECK	docile
RAVAGE	regret
HEINOUS	innards
QUIBBLE	badger
APPEASE	disagree
PASSIVE	plant eating

Egg Salad
Serves 4

8 eggs
½ cup minced white onion
¼ cup sour cream
1 tsp garlic powder
2 tbsp extra virgin olive oil
Salt and freshly ground black pepper to taste

Place the eggs in a pot, cover with water, place on a high heat and cover until hardboiled (the time depends on the altitude at which you cook; about 15 minutes at sea level).

Once boiled, remove the eggs from the heat, drain the water, and place in a bowl with cold water and ice. Allow the eggs to cool completely, about 5 minutes.

Peel the eggs, slice lengthwise in ½ and add to a medium bowl. Mix in the onion, olive oil, garlic powder, sour cream and a pinch of salt and pepper. Mash the mixture with a potato masher until desired consistency.

Serve on cucumber, bread, or crackers.

Calling the high protein egg dish a "salad" can only be meant as a DECOY since "salad" typically refers to foods grown in VERDANT fields. CONSCIENTIOUS LEXICOGRAPHERS seeking RIGOROUS standards for the dictionary are RELUCTANT to permit "egg salad" to be listed without a FOOTNOTE. This is how they REDRESS what they view as an effort to HOODWINK the public. Chefs can easily solve this NOSTRUM by placing the eggs on a bed of lettuce and tomatoes!

DECOY	scheme
VERDANT	exhaustive
CONSCIENTIOUS	deceive
LEXICOGRAPHER	snare
RIGOROUS	unwilling
RELUCTANT	thorough
FOOTNOTE	remedy
REDRESS	lush
HOODWINK	person compiling dictionaries
NOSTRUM	comment

Poached Salmon With Dill Yogurt Sauce
Serves 3

Salmon:
2 lbs cleaned, deboned salmon (skin on)
6½ cups water
6 large garlic cloves
1 small white onion
1 lemon
4 dill stalks
1 tsp salt + extra for taste
1 tsp pepper + extra to taste

Dill Yogurt Sauce:
⅓ cup Greek yogurt
4 tbsp minced dill + extra sprigs for garnish
½ lemon, juiced

Sliver the garlic and thinly slice the onion and lemon.

For the salmon: cut the salmon into three 2" x 6" pieces. Combine the water, garlic, onion, lemon, dill, salt, and pepper in a large pot on a high heat. Once this comes to a rolling boil, reduce the heat to a gentle simmer. Let the ingredients infuse the water for about 10 minutes.

Add the salmon, raise the heat to high and cover. Cook for 2 minutes, then reduce the heat to medium - low and cook for another 4 minutes. Remove from the pot and sprinkle with salt and pepper.

For the dill yogurt sauce: combine the yogurt, minced dill, and lemon juice and mix well. Pour over the salmon.

Garnish with dill sprigs.

Serve.

Poaching is a PROCEDURE that is AMENABLE to the PREPARATION of FRAGILE food such as eggs and fish. Water, wine, stock and VIRTUALLY any liquid that is not UNCTUOUS can be used as the "court bouillon," or poaching medium. Poaching is a SUBTLE process that is CONDITIONAL upon RESTRAINT. Key steps to success include: simmer (don't boil) and MINIMIZE poaching time.

PROCEDURE	control
AMENABLE	dependent
PREPARATION	delicate
FRAGILE	lessen
VIRTUALLY	oily
UNCTUOUS	accommodating
SUBTLE	breakable
CONDITIONAL	production
RESTRAINT	basically
MINIMIZE	process

Stuffed Peppers
Serves 4

1 cup cooked white rice
4 bell peppers, any color
6 baby bella mushrooms
1 sausage, any type
1 (7 oz) can diced tomatoes
4 tbsp plain canned tomato sauce
1 tbsp garlic powder
2 tbsp extra virgin olive oil
Salt and freshly ground black pepper to taste

Preheat the oven to 350° Fahrenheit.

Chop the tops off of the peppers and clean the insides. Dice the remaining flesh from the tops of the peppers. Dice the mushrooms and sausage.

Heat 1 tbsp of oil on a medium heat and sauté the tops of the peppers with the mushrooms for 5 - 7 minutes. Add the sausage and cook for another 3 minutes. Season the vegetables with salt and pepper. Set aside.

In a bowl, mix together the rice, tomatoes, cooked vegetables and sausage. Set aside.

Place the peppers in a baking dish and evenly drizzle the remaining oil on each pepper. Fill each pepper with ¼ of the rice mixture. Spread 1 tbsp of the sauce on top of each pepper.

Bake for about 50 minutes and serve.

Many food fanatics make the PRESUMPTION that stuffed peppers grew in popularity as people accumulated a HORDE of leftovers and didn't know what to do with them. What is known, is that peppers become loaded with a BOUILLABAISSE of tasty flavorings that improve when slightly SINGED in the oven. The SERPENTINE sausage can be made from HEIFER, chicken BOSOM, or BOVINE and PORCINE products. The thought of what went into this great stuffing for peppers may make you NAUSEOUS!

PRESUMPTION	sick
HORDE	young cow
BOUILLABAISSE	relating to pigs
SINGE	stew
SERPENTINE	throng
HEIFER	breast
BOSOM	relating to cows/cattle
BOVINE	snake-like
PORCINE	assumption
NAUSEOUS	lightly burn

Étouffée
Serves 4

1½ lbs shelled shrimp
1 small zucchini or yellow squash
½ cup diced white onion
1 green bell pepper
½ cup diced tomato
2 stalks celery
½ cup diced green onion
3 cups broth, any type
½ stick unsalted butter
3½ tbsp flour
¼ tsp cayenne
1 tsp Cajun seasoning
Salt and freshly ground black pepper to taste

Clean and devein the shrimp. Dice the celery, bell pepper and zucchini/squash.

In a large pot, melt the butter on a medium heat. Add the flour and cook for about 8 minutes, stirring continuously. Add the zucchini/squash, onion, bell pepper, tomato, celery, a pinch of salt and pepper, and cook, stirring occasionally, for about 10 minutes.

Add the green onion, broth, cayenne and Cajun seasoning and cook for another 2 minutes. Reduce the heat to low and simmer for about 30 minutes, stirring occasionally. Add the shrimp, stir, and cook for about 7 minutes or until cooked through.

Serve over rice.

"Étouffée" is French for "smother" and refers to a dish that features rice DRENCHED in a SUPERABUNDANCE of CRUSTACEANS and other proteins and vegetables. A CURSORY examination of the dish may mistake it for gumbo because both are OCHER, but with careful inspection one can CRYSTALLIZE their difference and DEDUCE that only gumbo is a soup. Spices insure that neither is INSIPID. This Cajun specialty has left its INDELIBLE mark on MASSIVE numbers of foodies.

DRENCH	infer
SUPERABUNDANCE	superficial
CRUSTACEAN	brownish
CURSORY	clarify
OCHER	excessive
CRYSTALLIZE	boring
DEDUCE	drown
INSIPID	aquatic arthropod
INDELIBLE	huge
MASSIVE	permanent

Polish Stuffed Cabbage
Makes 10 cabbage rolls

Cabbage:
1 large head of Savoy cabbage
3 cups ground meat, any kind
1 small bell pepper, any color
1½ cups cooked white rice
1 small white onion
2 eggs
4 cups water
Salt and freshly ground black
pepper to taste

Sauce:
1 (28 oz) can crushed tomatoes
1½ cups broth or water
¼ cup ketchup
1 lemon, juiced
1 tbsp granulated sugar
Hot sauce to taste (optional)

Finely chop the bell pepper and onion.

For the cabbage: remove the outer layer of the cabbage and core it from the bottom. Bring the water to a boil in a large pot. Add the whole head of cabbage and cook on high, covered, for about 8 minutes. Drain the water and let the cabbage cool completely before handling.

Meanwhile, combine the meat, bell pepper, rice, onion, eggs and a pinch of salt and pepper. Gently peel off 10 layers of cabbage. Save the rest for another recipe. Add 1/10 of the meat to the center of the cabbage leaf, roll in the sides first and then roll the length. Once you have completed all the rolls, set aside.

For the sauce: combine all of the sauce ingredients, making sure to leave 1 cup of the broth for the pot. Place ½ of the sauce in the bottom of the pot and then place the cabbage seam-side down. Try and fit the cabbage rolls snugly together. It's okay if you have to stack the rolls on top of each other. Place the rest of the sauce on top and spread with the remaining 1 cup of broth.

Cook, covered, on a high heat for 15 minutes. Reduce the heat to a gentle simmer and cook for another 45 minutes.

Serve.

Stuffed cabbage is a LEGACY of people with Polish HERITAGE. PARE the outside leaves of the cabbage and then boil. Once slightly soft, add SEASONAL fillings, and STEEP in the boiling liquid. Poles with PARAMOUNT PATRIOTISM can be CONTENDERS in "Gołąbki" eating contests. The winner might feel PHLEGMATIC after SUFFERING the effects of a postprandial alkaline tide, the fatigue that comes after eating a big meal. These filling rolls are not for the faint hearted.

LEGACY	fluctuating by time of year
HERITAGE	troubled by
PARE	rival
SEASONAL	supreme
STEEP	placid
PARAMOUNT	birthright
PATRIOTISM	allegiance
CONTENDER	bequest
PHLEGMATIC	soak
SUFFER	remove

Tofu Enchiladas
Serves 4

1 (12 oz) package of extra firm tofu, frozen
1 cup shredded Monterey Jack cheese
1 small white onion
1 cup of enchilada sauce
Zest and juice of 1 lime
4 - 6 corn tortillas
Jalapeño pepper slices (from a jar)
1 small can sliced black olives
8 sprigs cilantro
½ tsp chili powder
Extra virgin olive oil
Salt to taste

Preheat the oven to 350° Fahrenheit.

Mince the onion.

Defrost the tofu in the microwave. Cut it in half lengthwise, squeeze as much water out of it as you can, then cut it into ½" cubes.

Sauté the tofu, onion and chili powder in a pan on a medium heat until golden. Combine with ¼ cup enchilada sauce, ½ cup cheese and lime juice in a large bowl.

Spread a thin layer of enchilada sauce (about ¼ cup) on the bottom of a casserole dish.

Spoon ¼ of the tofu mixture onto the center of each tortilla. Top each with 3 - 5 jalapeño pepper slices. Roll the tortillas and place them tightly side-by-side in the casserole dish. Cover the tortillas with the rest of the enchilada sauce and cheese. Bake for 30 minutes.

Remove from the oven and garnish with slices of olives and cilantro sprigs.

Serve.

Those who THEORIZE about the origin of tofu would have to DEVISE a pie chart and TRISECT it to EVINCE proposals that demonstrate AUTHENTICITY. The first theory holds that a Chinese prince invented it, but scholars CRITIQUE that view by pointing out that the product was too INCHOATE to be considered modern day tofu. The second theory holds that tofu was found by accident, a result of mixing ground soybeans with ADULTERATED sea salt. The final theory is that Chinese SCOUNDRELS stole the technique from Mongolians. The original EXEMPLAR for tofu remains unknown.

THEORIZE	analyze
DEVISE	genuineness
TRISECT	indicate
EVINCE	invent
AUTHENTICITY	alter
CRITIQUE	model
INCHOATE	divide into 3
ADULTERATE	rascal
SCOUNDREL	hypothesize
EXEMPLAR	undeveloped

Ruby's Belizean Red Beans
Serves 5

8 oz red kidney beans
28 cups water
2 stalks celery
1 red bell pepper
8 garlic cloves
1 tsp pepper
1 tsp garlic powder
1 tsp ground rosemary
1 tsp thyme
1 tsp garlic salt
1 tsp rubbed sage
1 tbsp salt + more to taste
1 small white onion
1 tbsp unsalted butter
2 tbsp extra virgin olive oil

Wash the kidney beans. Cut the celery stalks lengthwise in half and chop into medium size pieces. Chop the bell pepper into small pieces. Mince the onion and garlic.

Place the beans in a large pot with 20 cups of water. Add the celery, bell pepper, minced garlic and all of the spices and oil. Cook uncovered on a high heat for 1 hour 15 minutes. Cover, add the remaining water and let cook for about 1 hour or until slightly thickened. Turn off the heat, remove the cover, stir, and let sit.

In a separate pan, cook the onion and butter on a medium heat for 7 minutes or until golden brown. Add the onion to the bean mixture. Cook uncovered for about 40 minutes, or until the beans have thickened. Season to taste with salt.

Serve over rice or in a tortilla.

Rice and beans are staple fare in Central and South America and the Caribbean, COURTESY of European and African settlers. Rice and beans are TEEMING with vitamins and COLLABORATE to provide all dietary essential amino acids, the building blocks which AGGREGATE into protein. Brown beans are HACKNEYED, so go red, a DISTINCTION that will make this meal AUTHENTICALLY Belizean. A NUANCE to be aware of: "rice and beans" DENOTE a dish with the ingredients served together, whereas the INVERSE, "beans and rice" indicate the two ingredients are served side by side.

COURTESY	sum
TEEMING	opposite
COLLABORATE	full of
AGGREGATE	overused
HACKNEYED	offered
DISTINCTION	genuine
AUTHENTIC	cooperate
NUANCE	indicate
DENOTE	subtlety
INVERSE	contrast

Breakfast For Dinner (Buttermilk Biscuit With Poached Egg Florentine)
Serves 10

Biscuits:
2 cups flour + extra for kneading
4 tsp baking powder
½ tsp baking soda
½ stick cold unsalted butter
1 cup cold buttermilk + extra for brushing
1 tsp salt

Spinach Florentine:
5 cups firmly packed baby spinach leaves
¼ cup milk
1 tbsp extra virgin olive oil
Salt to taste

Poached Eggs:
10 eggs
Water
¼ cup white vinegar

Preheat the oven to 450° Fahrenheit.

Cube the butter.

For the biscuits: place the flour, baking powder, baking soda, and salt in a bowl. Mix in the butter quickly until it resembles coarse crumbs. This works well in a food processor. Mix in the buttermilk and place the dough on a floured surface. Fold the dough over itself a few times, then roll it out until it's about 1" in thickness. Use a 2" cookie cutter to make the biscuits. If you have any scraps, roll them up and keep making biscuits (these won't be as good). Place them on a baking sheet and brush with milk. Bake for about 17 minutes.

For the poached eggs: fill a medium pot with water and the vinegar. Bring to a gentle simmer on a medium heat. Crack 1 egg at a time into a small bowl and gently slide it into the water. It is important to have no more than 3 eggs in the water at a time. Cook for about 2 - 3 minutes.

Meanwhile, place the spinach in a pan with the oil on a medium heat, and cook for a few minutes or until the spinach is wilted. Add the milk and cook for a few more minutes or until the milk is reduced and thickened. Salt to taste.

Arrange an egg and spinach on each biscuit and serve.

The term "buttermilk" is a bit of a MISNOMER since it is not COMPRISED of butter and has a thicker CONSISTENCY than milk. The process of churning butter creates a RESIDUE that we know as "buttermilk." A simpler method of production is to ACIDIFY milk by adding white vinegar or lemon juice. Buttermilk won't QUALIFY as a CONTEMPORARY favorite in the ANNALS of great drinks, but even those who shudder at the thought of IMBIBING it can ACKNOWLEDGE its value in baking.

MISNOMER	remainder
COMPRISE	records
CONSISTENCY	change into acid
RESIDUE	wrong name
ACIDIFY	consist of
QUALIFY	modern
CONTEMPORARY	density
ANNALS	drink
IMBIBE	recognize
ACKNOWLEDGE	be eligible

Vegetable Pot Pie
Serves 4 - 5

1 bell pepper, any color
8 oz white mushrooms
1 large white onion
2 stalks celery
⅔ cup frozen corn kernels
⅔ cup frozen peas
3 peeled carrots
⅓ cup + 2 tbsp flour + more for rolling
1½ cup broth, any kind
1 cup whole milk
2 sheets store bought puff pastry
3 tbsp unsalted butter
1½ tsp salt
1 tsp pepper
¼ tsp cayenne pepper
2 tbsp extra virgin olive oil
Nonstick cooking spray

Preheat the oven to 400° Fahrenheit. Spray the bottom of a large casserole dish with cooking spray.

Chop the bell pepper, celery, carrots, onion and mushrooms into ½" chunks. Melt the butter and oil in a large pan on a medium - high heat. Add the bell pepper, mushrooms, onion, celery, corn, salt, pepper, and cayenne. Cook for 10 minutes, stirring occasionally. Reduce the heat to low and add the peas, carrots and flour, stir, and cook for one minute. Add the broth and milk, stir, and cook for about 4 minutes or until the mixture thickens. Set aside.

Flour a surface and roll out 1 sheet of the puff pastry until it becomes an 11" x 11" square. Place it in the casserole dish and prick it with a fork. It's okay if the edges hang over the side and it doesn't completely cover the dish. Bake for about 7 - 9 minutes, or until golden brown.

Add the filling, cover with the other sheet of unrolled puff pastry and let the edges of the pastry hang over the sides. Score in the middle, and bake for about 35 minutes or until golden brown.

Serve immediately.

Pot pie is a meal ENCASED in a flaky crust. It is REPUTED to be a favorite of PROLETARIANS, an UNTOWARD reputation that UNDERSTATES its contribution to culinary arts. Pot pie holds a REVERENT POSITION in the REPERTORY of hearty cuisine. All-in-one foods are a reminder of the PIONEER spirit, an INDOMITABLE force that made our country great.

ENCASE	founding
REPUTED	humble
PROLETARIAN	spot
UNTOWARD	collection
UNDERSTATE	enclose
REVERENT	unconquerable
POSITION	underplay
REPERTORY	annoying
PIONEER	low-class
INDOMITABLE	said

Turkey Tostada
Serves 2

2 flat tostada shells
¼ cup canned black beans
4 tbsp cooked corn kernels (you can use canned corn)
1 small tomato
2 tbsp diced red onion
¼ cup diced, cooked turkey
¼ cup grated sharp cheddar cheese
3 chives
2 tbsp lime juice
¼ cup sour cream
½ cup shredded lettuce
1 tbsp minced fresh cilantro
Hot sauce to taste
Salt and freshly ground black pepper to taste

Rinse, drain and pat dry the black beans. Dice the tomato. Mince the chives.

In a small bowl, combine the chives, lime juice, sour cream, lettuce, cilantro, hot sauce, and a pinch of salt and pepper. Scoop the mixture evenly onto each tostada shell.

Top with black beans, corn, tomato, onion, turkey and cheddar cheese.

Serve.

Tostadas were discovered by people who wished to AMELIORATE the WANTON practice of wasting food. Tortillas, made by the SUBMERSION of dough in boiling oil, quickly became stale if uneaten, an unaffordable EXTRAVAGANCE. It was found, almost as an AFTERTHOUGHT, that ARID conditions transformed the tortilla into the longer lasting tostada. This bred a group of ITINERANT farmers who could AMBULATE INLAND in search of the most ARABLE conditions.

AMELIORATE	walk
WANTON	landlocked
SUBMERSION	moving
EXTRAVAGANCE	reckless
AFTERTHOUGHT	luxury
ARID	farmable
ITINERANT	dry
AMBULATE	plunged below
INLAND	reconsideration
ARABLE	improve

Gourmet Grilled Cheese
Serves 1

2 slices sourdough bread
1 slice American cheese
1 slice cheddar cheese
1 tbsp goat cheese
1 tbsp unsalted butter, softened

Place a pan on a medium heat.

Evenly spread the butter on one side of each slice of bread. Place 1 slice, butter side down, on the pan. Spread on the goat cheese. Add the American and cheddar slices. Cover with the other slice of bread. Make sure to have the top slice, butter-side up.

Flip after a few minutes and cook for another few minutes, until each side is golden brown.

Serve.

Rabbi Hillel has RIGHTFUL POSSESSION of the DESIGNATION of inventor of the sandwich, which, at INCEPTION, was open-faced and made with matzoh. His MEMORABLE contribution is paid HOMAGE every year by including a "Hillel sandwich" in the seder meal, in OBSERVANCE of Passover. The sandwich, as it is known in MODERNITY, is credited to the DEBONAIR Earl of Sandwich, who had no time for sit-down dinners because he was too ENTHUSED with gambling.

———

RIGHTFUL	noteworthy
POSSESSION	eager
DESIGNATION	ownership
INCEPTION	celebration
MEMORABLE	appellation
HOMAGE	present
OBSERVANCE	charming
MODERNITY	legitimate
DEBONAIR	acknowledgment
ENTHUSED	beginning

Dessert

Raspberry Lemon L-7s (Raspberry Lemon Squares)
Cinnamon Apple Strudel With Cinnamon Whipped Cream
Strawberry Rhubarb Crostata
Nectarine Blueberry Crumble With Oatmeal Topping
Sweet Potato Soufflé
Cheesecake With Nut Crust
Tiramisu
Chocolate Avocado Pudding
Zucchini Brownies
Banana Bread
Cinnamon Crème Anglaise Ice Cream
Pistachio Ice Cream
Watermelon Granita
Carrot Cake
Chocolate Cake With Mocha Buttercream
Fruit Tart With Graham Cracker Crust
Orange Cranberry Muffins
Nutella (Chocolate And Hazelnut) Biscotti
Nougat
White Chocolate Bark
Baklava
Dulce De Leche Pudding
Orange Tea Infused Hot Chocolate
Ginger Scones
Cinnamon Rolls
Shortbread Cookies Dipped In Chocolate
Chocolate Chip Cookies
Molasses Cookies
Apple Rhubarb Sauce
Fruit Parfait
Poached Pears
Grilled Peaches With Vanilla Mascarpone
Gourmet Banana Split Sundae

Raspberry Lemon L-7s (Raspberry Lemon Squares)
Makes 16 (2" bars)

Shortbread:
1 stick unsalted butter, softened to room temperature
¼ cup sugar
1 cup flour
⅛ tsp salt
Nonstick cooking spray or unsalted butter

Lemon Filling:
15 raspberries
1 cup sugar
3 eggs
2 tbsp flour
Zest of 1 lemon
2 lemons, juiced
Powdered sugar

Preheat the oven to 350° Fahrenheit.

For the shortbread: cream the butter, sugar, and salt. This is best done with an electric hand mixer or stand mixer. Slowly beat in the flour. Grease an 8" x 8" baking pan. Spread the dough into the bottom of the pan, making sure to cover all of the corners. Bake for about 18 minutes. Remove from the oven and allow it to cool.

For the lemon filling: mince the raspberries. Beat the sugar and eggs until smooth. Add the lemon juice, zest, and flour. Fold in the raspberries. Pour onto the crust and bake for another 18 - 20 minutes or until the filling has just set. Remove from the oven and let cool completely. Dust with powdered sugar and cut into squares.

Serve.

"L 7" is an ANACHRONISM, retro slang for a "square." Use this GESTURE to DEMONSTRATE the meaning: create an "L" with your left thumb and forefinger and an upside down "L," otherwise known as a "7," with your right thumb and forefinger. Merge them and they magically COALESCE into a square. In COLLOQUIAL use, the term "square" will IMPUGN a PARAGON of CONFORMITY, one who could benefit by some IMPETUOSITY. Lemon L-7s, known as "lemon squares" in common PARLANCE, are delicious regardless of their controversial shape.

ANACHRONISM	example
GESTURE	attack
DEMONSTRATE	speech
COALESCE	motion
COLLOQUIAL	impulsive
IMPUGN	show
PARAGON	old-fashioned
CONFORMITY	informal
IMPETUOUS	compliance
PARLANCE	combine

Cinnamon Apple Strudel With Cinnamon Whipped Cream
Serves 6 - 8

Apple Strudel:
2 medium Granny Smith apples
3 tbsp apple juice
¼ cup sugar
1 tbsp flour
1 tsp cinnamon
2 tsp vanilla extract
1 sheet store bought puff pastry

Cinnamon Whipped Cream:
¾ cup whipping cream
2 tbsp powdered sugar
½ tsp cinnamon
½ tsp vanilla

Egg Wash:
1 egg
1 tbsp water

Preheat the oven to 375° Fahrenheit.

For the apple strudel: peel, core and thinly slice the apples. Combine the apple juice, sugar, flour, cinnamon and vanilla extract in a medium bowl. Add the apples and mix well.

Sprinkle flour lightly on a cutting board. Gently unroll the puff pastry and cover it with a light sprinkle of flour. Roll out the puff pastry on the board to a 12" x 14" sheet. Cover half of the puff pastry with the apple mixture, leaving a 1" border on all sides. Do not add any fluid from the mixture. Starting at the border, roll the puff pastry all the way to the other end. Tuck in the short ends of the log.

For the egg wash: beat the egg and water and lightly brush onto the strudel log with a pastry brush.

Score the strudel log diagonally with a sharp knife. Each score should be 1½" in length and 2" apart, a total of 4 scores. Spray a 12" baking pan with nonstick cooking spray. Place the strudel log in the pan and bake for 30 - 35 minutes.

For the cinnamon whipped cream: beat the whipping cream for 2 minutes, then add the cinnamon, vanilla and powdered sugar and beat an extra minute, or until stiff peaks form. This is best done in a stand mixer or electric hand mixer.

Cool and slice the apple strudel and serve with whipped cream.

Apple strudel, a rich and LUSCIOUS dessert, EVOKES the Austro-Hungarian Empire from which it came. Imagine CONNOISSEURS of food and wine clothed in majestic attire, served in OPULENT sitting rooms, REGALING in GLUTTONY with no concern for the INEVITABLE outcome. These CORPULENT individuals might have been more mindful of the benefits of ABSTINENCE! MODERATION will allow you to enjoy this sinful pleasure without worrying about your waistline.

LUSCIOUS	expert
EVOKE	delight
CONNOISSEUR	fat
OPULENT	temperance
REGALE	summon
GLUTTONY	luxurious
INEVITABLE	refraining
CORPULENT	rich
ABSTINENCE	predictable
MODERATION	overeating

Strawberry Rhubarb Crostata
Serves 6

Dough:
1 cup flour + more for rolling
1 stick cold unsalted butter
2 tbsp sugar
2 tbsp ice water
¼ tsp salt

Filling:
1 cup hulled, quartered strawberries
1 cup diced rhubarb
4 tbsp sugar

Preheat the oven to 450° Fahrenheit.

For the dough: cube the butter. Combine the flour, sugar, and salt in a food processor and pulse a few times. Add the butter and pulse until it resembles small peas. With the mixer running, pour in the water and mix until just combined. Turn out the dough onto a sheet of plastic wrap and quickly form it into about a 6" disk. Place it in the refrigerator for at least 1 hour.

Roll out the dough to an 11" circle and transfer it to a baking dish.

For the filling: combine the strawberries, rhubarb, and sugar in a bowl and mix well.

Add the strawberries and rhubarb to the center of the dough round, leaving a 2" border all around. Raise the dough over the fruit and pleat, making sure to overlap the dough. Pinch the pleats.

Place the crostata in the oven and bake for about 20 - 25 minutes. After 12 minutes, check the crostata to make sure the crust isn't burning. If it is, loosely place a sheet of tin foil over the top and keep baking.

Serve with vanilla ice cream.

A crostata is a baked dessert tart. COLLEGIANS might define "tart" as "sour" or "ASTRINGENT," but PHILOLOGISTS remind us that a word can have more than one SENSE. USAGE of the term in fruit "tart" IMPLIES a food VARIANT of pie. To DISPEL any confusion about this WHOLLY different meaning, repeat these words VERBATIM when discussing crostata, "Place a filling in a pastry base and bake."

COLLEGIAN	alternative
ASTRINGENT	language expert
PHILOLOGIST	college student
SENSE	eliminate
USAGE	exactly
IMPLY	entirely
VARIANT	meaning
DISPEL	indicate
WHOLLY	harsh
VERBATIM	treatment

Nectarine Blueberry Crumble With Oatmeal Topping

Serves 5 - 6

Fruit Filling:
4 ripe nectarines
12 oz blueberries
¼ cup orange juice
2 tbsp granulated sugar
3 tbsp packed light brown sugar
1 tbsp cornstarch

Crumble Topping:
⅓ cup flour
⅓ cup granulated sugar
⅔ cup instant rolled oats + ¼ cup
1 stick cold unsalted butter, diced

Preheat the oven to 375° Fahrenheit.

For the fruit filling: chop the nectarines into ½" thick slices. Combine all of the ingredients for the fruit filling mixture. Place in a round 9" pan.

For the crumble topping: mix together the ingredients for the topping, making sure to save the ¼ cup of the oats. It is best to use a food processor, but if you don't have one, use your hands to incorporate the butter into the dough.

Place the crumble on top of the fruit. It's okay if the crumble chunks are large. Sprinkle the rest of the oats on top and bake for 45 minutes - 1 hour, or until the top is golden brown.

Serve.

Goldilocks, the IMPULSIVE little girl in the beloved childhood fairy tale, was never EXPLICIT about the type of porridge she nibbled in the DOMICILE of those three HOSPITABLE and PROPITIOUS bears. "Porridge" is a GENERIC term for a hot dish made by boiling cereal, grains or legumes in milk or water. Oatmeal is a specific type of porridge, and we can EXTRAPOLATE from the story that it was the breakfast that the VAGRANT PROTAGONIST stumbled upon during her PERIPATETIC adventure.

IMPULSIVE	gather
EXPLICIT	spontaneous
DOMICILE	wandering
HOSPITABLE	roaming
PROPITIOUS	welcoming
GENERIC	clear
EXTRAPOLATE	kindly
VAGRANT	main character
PROTAGONIST	common
PERIPATETIC	home

Sweet Potato Soufflé
Serves 10

Soufflé:
6 small sweet potatoes
2 cups heavy whipping cream
1 cup light cream
2 tsp cinnamon
1 tsp nutmeg
½ cup light brown sugar, packed

Topping:
¾ cup Irish oats
½ cup cashews
1 tsp cinnamon
1 tsp nutmeg
1 tsp vanilla
¼ cup light brown sugar, packed
3 tbsp unsalted butter, melted
1 tbsp coconut oil

Preheat the oven to 375° Fahrenheit.

For the soufflé: cut the sweet potatoes in half lengthwise. Place the potatoes on a sheet pan and bake for 1 hour or until soft. Scoop out the potato meat from the skin and place it in a food processor or blender. Add the whipping cream, light cream, cinnamon, nutmeg, and brown sugar. Place the mixture in a buttered 8" x 8" square dish. Set aside.

For the topping: combine all of the topping ingredients in a food processor and pulse until granular. Distribute the mixture evenly on the sweet potatoes and cover tightly with tin foil.

Place in the oven and bake for 40 minutes.

Cool for 10 minutes before serving.

Until the 1950s, coconut oil was a pantry staple. After a scientific study ENCOURAGED nixing it due to PERNICIOUS saturated fats, the use of the anything-but-BANAL oil ABRUPTLY DESISTED. For a while, coconut oil seemed NONEXISTENT, but scientists continued experimenting and found that a new VERSION, "virgin coconut oil," had the POTENTIAL to be just as flavorful, while providing healthy fats. The REVIVAL of coconut oil was a FORMIDABLE undertaking that finally returned it to local supermarkets and specialty food stores.

ENCOURAGE	commonplace
PERNICIOUS	sudden
BANAL	impressive
ABRUPT	form
DESIST	harmful
NONEXISTENT	reawakening
VERSION	absent
POTENTIAL	cease
REVIVAL	capacity
FORMIDABLE	inspire

Cheesecake With Nut Crust
Serves 12

Filling:	Zest of 1 lemon	Crust:
32 oz cream cheese, softened to room temperature	1 tsp vanilla extract	3 cups shelled walnuts
1 cup sour cream	4 eggs	4 tbsp sugar
1 cup sugar	Water	
½ lemon, juiced	Unsalted butter for greasing the pan	

Preheat the oven to 350° Fahrenheit.

Butter a 9" spring form pan.

For the crust: in a food processor or blender, combine the walnuts and sugar and process or blend until the oils start to release from the walnuts. You will know that it's done when it starts to come together and resemble a crust. Press the nut crust into the bottom of the spring form pan to create a smooth layer. Bake for about 15 minutes.

For the filling: combine the cream cheese, sour cream, sugar, juice, zest, and vanilla. Slowly beat in the eggs. This process works best in a stand mixer or electric hand mixer. Place this mixture on top of the crust.

Wrap the outside and underside of the spring form pan with aluminum foil to prevent any water from touching the cheesecake. Place the pan in another baking dish and fill it with water so it reaches about ½ way up the spring form pan. Bake for about 15 minutes.

Reduce the heat to 250° Fahrenheit and continue baking for about 1½ hours. Immediately take the cheesecake out of the water and remove the tin foil. Let it cool completely at room temperature.

Refrigerate the cake for about 2 hours. To release the cake from the pan, run a knife between the cake and the pan and then release.

Slice and serve.

Although cream cheese seems like a spread, by definition, it's categorized as a cheese. Don't be DECEIVED by the brand, "Philadelphia," because cream cheese originated in France and later New York, where it was DENOMINATED. FERVID cream cheese lovers who wish to abandon the HABITUAL can CONFRONT their DARING side by choosing to ESCHEW the NORM and try Boursin and mascarpone, fun ways to APPRECIATE an ABERRATION.

DECEIVE	enjoy
DENOMINATE	mislead
FERVID	standard
HABITUAL	audacious
CONFRONT	name
DARING	escape
ESCHEW	passionate
NORM	deviation
APPRECIATE	constant
ABERRATION	challenge

Tiramisu

Serves 8 - 10

1 cup + 4 tbsp brewed espresso
¼ cup heavy whipping cream
30 ladyfingers
6 egg yolks
5 tbsp sugar
1 tsp vanilla
14 oz mascarpone cheese
1 tbsp cocoa powder

Allow the espresso to cool.

Using an electric mixer, whip the cream on high until stiff peaks form.

In a bowl, whisk together the egg yolks, sugar, and vanilla until thick and pale yellow. It's best to use an electric mixer. Add the mascarpone and 4 tbsp espresso and whisk until smooth. Gently fold in the whipped cream and then set the mixture aside.

To assemble the tiramisu, dip ½ of the ladyfingers in the coffee and let soak for about 3 - 5 seconds. Place in a small - medium casserole dish. Top with ½ of the cream. Sift half of the cocoa powder over the cream. Repeat this process again 1 more time to complete the tiramisu.

Cover with plastic wrap and refrigerate for at least 2 hours before serving.

Tiramisu, an Italian dessert, is a favorite among the culinary BROTHERHOOD. The origin of this dish is subject to SPECULATION but most of the ASSERTIONS are DUBIOUS. A brothel, bakers, and chefs are among the many CLAIMANTS who take credit, but the truth is EQUIVOCAL. To make this confection, IMMERSE biscuits in coffee, arrange in a LATTICE formation, layer with sweet cream, and dust with cocoa. EXPRESSIVE guests will shout "EUREKA!" to show appreciation.

BROTHERHOOD	applicant
SPECULATION	statement
ASSERTION	bingo
DUBIOUS	fellowship
CLAIMANT	doubtful
EQUIVOCAL	intertwining
IMMERSE	conjecture
LATTICE	submerge
EXPRESSIVE	unclear
EUREKA	passionate

Chocolate Avocado Pudding
Serves 2

1 ripe banana
1 ripe avocado
2 - 3 tbsp unsweetened cocoa powder + more to taste
1 tbsp honey + more to taste

Mix all of the ingredients in a food processor, blender, stand mixer, or in a bowl with a wire whisk. Combine until the mixture reaches a smooth, pudding-like consistency. Add more cocoa and honey if needed.

Refrigerate.

Serve chilled.

Avocado pudding you ask? Don't allow your reaction to this odd combination to DETER its exploration in your kitchen. Even a RECALCITRANT eater who DETESTS fruit will find this to be a most satisfying COMESTIBLE. COMMINGLE the avocado and cocoa powder to create a recipe that celebrates INGENUITY while MAINTAINING the same texture and color as the traditional gelatinous treat. Top with fresh berries or slices of bananas to CONSUMMATE the dessert. The AMALGAM of avocado, banana, honey, and cocoa powder creates a truly GASTRONOMIC experience.

DETER	blend
RECALCITRANT	inventiveness
DETEST	mixture
COMESTIBLE	uncooperative
COMMINGLE	conserve
INGENUITY	food
MAINTAIN	appetizing
CONSUMMATE	discourage
AMALGAM	complete
GASTRONOMIC	loathe

Zucchini Brownies
Serves 14 - 16

1 small zucchini
2 eggs
1 tsp vanilla extract
1 stick unsalted butter, melted
¼ tsp baking powder
1 cup sugar
½ cup flour
¼ tsp salt
⅓ cup unsweetened cocoa powder
3 milk chocolate bars (optional)
Nonstick cooking spray

Preheat the oven to 350° Fahrenheit.

Grease a 13" x 9" pan with nonstick cooking spray. Grate the zucchini.

Mix together the wet ingredients. Add the dry ingredients to the wet, and whisk well to combine. Mix in the grated zucchini. Pour half of the brownie batter into the prepared pan.

Place the 3 chocolate bars side by side on top of the batter in the pan, but don't press down. Add the rest of the batter on top and bake for 27 - 30 minutes.

Let the brownies cool before cutting and serving.

If you CONCEDE that baking zucchini in a dessert seems PREPOSTEROUS, it may well be that your BIAS is against IRREVERENCE. Adding a vegetable to a sweet is AUDACIOUS, but it is also INDICATIVE of a willingness to be RECEPTIVE to new ideas. As an ingredient in brownies, shredded or grated zucchini is NEUTRAL in flavor while adding moisture and an airy texture. Abandon your SKEPTICISM and give these treats a try . . . you may become their biggest ADVOCATE!

CONCEDE	responsive
PREPOSTEROUS	disrespect
BIAS	defender
IRREVERENCE	nonaligned
AUDACIOUS	doubt
INDICATIVE	absurd
RECEPTIVE	suggestive
NEUTRAL	fearless
SKEPTICISM	favoritism
ADVOCATE	surrender

Banana Bread
Serves 8

¾ cup mashed ripe banana (about 2 bananas)
2 eggs
¼ cup milk
1 tsp vanilla extract
½ cup vegetable or canola oil
1 cup granulated sugar (+ ¼ cup more for sweeter bread)
1½ cups flour + extra for the pan
½ cup chopped walnuts/pecans
¾ tsp baking powder
1 tsp baking soda
Unsalted butter

Preheat the oven to 350° Fahrenheit.

Lightly butter a 9" x 5" loaf pan.

Combine the banana, eggs, milk, vanilla and oil in a bowl. Stir in the dry ingredients and add the nuts.

Bake for about 45 minutes or until a toothpick inserted comes out clean.

Let the bread cool completely before removing from the pan.

Slice and serve.

Neanderthals roaming the earth 12,000 years ago introduced a very PRIMITIVE form of bread. Historians are SKEPTICAL as to how these PRIMEVAL beings were able to bake. Many INFER that crushed grains and water were mixed and cooked on a TORRID stone. Today, bread is a food that can be served with many ACCOUTERMENTS, including bananas. Bananas are recognized for their CONSPICUOUS taste and pleasantly ODOROUS scent, but are less well known for causing a SOMNIFEROUS state, so try banana bread if you suffer from INSOMNIA.

PRIMITIVE	sleeplessness
SKEPTICAL	crude
PRIMEVAL	sleeping
INFER	hot
TORRID	fragrant
ACCOUTERMENT	doubting
CONSPICUOUS	accessory
ODOROUS	conclude
SOMNIFEROUS	ancient
INSOMNIA	apparent

Cinnamon Crème Anglaise Ice Cream
Serves 4

4 egg yolks
½ cup sugar
1 tsp cinnamon
1 tsp vanilla
1 cup whole milk
1 cup light cream

In a stand mixer on high, beat the egg yolks, sugar, cinnamon and vanilla for about 2 minutes until the mixture is a light lemon color.

Scald the milk and cream on a low heat in a small pot. The milk mixture should form little bubbles around the edge of the pot. Slowly pour the milk mixture into the egg mixture and whisk vigorously. Be careful to pour the milk extra slowly so the yolks don't scramble.
Place this mixture back into the pot on a low simmer. Stir continuously for 8 - 10 minutes. The mixture should reach between 160° and 170° Fahrenheit, but no more.

Once slightly thickened, immediately transfer the pot to an ice bath and let it cool completely.

Following the manufacturer's instructions, churn the ice cream mixture in an ice cream maker and then transfer it to a plastic container.

Freeze for at least 3 hours and serve.

Crème Anglaise, which TRANSLATES to "English custard," is a common French sauce that is served over meringues, cookies, as a base for ice cream, or eaten by itself. The sauce is made by whipping egg yolks and sugar, then adding scalded milk in a PIECEMEAL fashion and cooking it over a low heat with a WEE amount of vanilla. This process can be LABORIOUS, but the result is SUPERB. You may feel CHAGRIN if the texture isn't correct; it may seem SPECIOUS that the milk will curdle in the process of cooking. A CIRCUMSPECT and AMBITIOUS person is required to make this PRECISE sauce delicious.

TRANSLATE	exact
PIECEMEAL	toilsome
WEE	excellent
LABORIOUS	annoyance
SUPERB	convert
CHAGRIN	tiny
SPECIOUS	misleading
CIRCUMSPECT	gradual
AMBITIOUS	cautious
PRECISE	aspiring

Pistachio Ice Cream
Makes 8 cups of ice cream

1 cup unsalted pistachios
1 cup sugar
½ tsp almond extract
1¾ cups whole milk
3 cups heavy cream
10 extra large egg yolks
3 tbsp cream cheese

Shell, finely chop and toast the pistachios (see "White Chocolate Bark" recipe for instructions on toasting nuts). Let them cool.

Mix together the pistachios, ¼ cup sugar and the almond extract. Set aside.

Bring the milk and cream to a gentle boil on a medium heat in a large pot. Set aside.

Mix together the egg yolks and the remaining sugar in a separate bowl. Add about ¼ cup of the hot mixture to the egg yolks and sugar. Do this about 4 times to bring up the temperature of the eggs. While constantly whisking, slowly pour the egg mixture into the pot of milk. Cook on a low heat for a few minutes or until the mixture reaches about 165° Fahrenheit and thickens. Immediately remove from the heat and strain into a bowl.

Add the sugar, pistachio, and almond mixture and stir. Place the bowl into an ice bath. Let the mixture cool completely.

Place in an ice cream maker with the cream cheese, and churn according to manufacturer's instructions.

Freeze for at least 3 hours in an airtight container before serving.

Have you ever heard of "The Pistachio Effect"? It's the concept that food tastes better when you have to work at eating it. If correct, this explains why the intense amount of DRUDGERY involved in shelling nuts makes people BELIEVE pistachios are exceptionally EXCELLENT. Other foods that benefit from this PHENOMENON are lobster, pomegranates and clams. "The Pistachio Effect" is most likely BOGUS, but NEVERTHELESS, these nuts have a FABULOUS taste and are worth the time you will EXPEND. Pistachios can be made into LIQUOR, ice cream or just eaten straight out of the bag. They are often sold in SPECIALTY shops.

DRUDGERY	spend
BELIEVE	labor
EXCELLENT	incredible
PHENOMENON	however
BOGUS	accept
NEVERTHELESS	distinctive
FABULOUS	alcohol
EXPEND	phony
LIQUOR	occurrence
SPECIALTY	outstanding

Watermelon Granita
Serves 5

4 cups chopped watermelon (about ½ - 1 small watermelon)
1 lemon, juiced (⅛ cup juice)
½ cup orange juice, no pulp
2 tbsp sugar

Combine all of the ingredients in a food processor. Process until the mixture becomes a liquid.

Using a fine mesh strainer, strain the watermelon mixture until there are only thick watermelon grounds left.

Discard the grounds and pour the watermelon juice into a freezable plastic dish and cover with plastic wrap.

Place in the freezer and scrape with a fork every hour for 3 – 4 hours.

Serve cold.

Granita is a GLACIAL Italian dessert made from FRIGID, shaved ice. Frozen liquid is scraped to SEPARATE crystals, thereby TRANSMUTING its chemical MAKEUP. A gelato machine can be used to smooth the texture. Alcohol, if added, can make one GIDDY and INEBRIATED. Granitas are common palate cleansers served between courses to ENERGIZE the taste buds in preparation for FURTHER NUTRIMENT.

GLACIAL	divide
FRIGID	composition
SEPARATE	arouse
TRANSMUTE	cold
MAKEUP	advance
GIDDY	drunk
INEBRIATED	change
ENERGIZE	nourishment
FURTHER	dizzy
NUTRIMENT	icy

Carrot Cake
Serves 8

Cake:
2 cups flour + more for the pans
3 eggs
4 oz softened cream cheese
½ cup extra virgin olive oil
1 cup granulated sugar
2 tsp baking powder
1 tsp baking soda
¼ tsp cinnamon
¼ tsp nutmeg

1 tbsp vanilla
½ tsp salt
1 cup tightly packed grated carrots (about 4 medium carrots)
¼ cup chopped walnuts or pecans + more for decoration
¼ cup sweetened coconut flakes + more for decoration
2 sticks softened unsalted butter + more for the pans

Frosting:
12 oz softened cream cheese
¾ cup granulated sugar
½ stick softened unsalted butter
1 tsp vanilla extract
¼ cup water

Preheat the oven to 350° Fahrenheit.

For the cake: using an electric hand mixer, cream the butter, olive oil and sugar. Add the eggs one at a time and mix on low. Add the cream cheese and keep mixing. Slowly incorporate the flour, baking powder, baking soda, salt, nutmeg, cinnamon and vanilla. Mix until just combined. Using a rubber spatula, mix in the carrots, nuts, and coconut flakes. Butter and flour two round 9" baking pans and evenly pour the batter into each pan. Bake for 30 minutes or until a toothpick inserted comes out clean. Cool completely and then remove from the pans.

For the frosting: combine all of the frosting ingredients and mix well. Once the cakes cool, spread frosting on one cake and then gently set the other on top to make a double layer cake. Frost the top of the second cake and the sides.

For optional decoration: sprinkle the coconut flakes on the top of the cake and the nuts on the sides.

Slice and serve.

Carrot cake, also known as "passion cake," dates back to the medieval EPOCH, when the supply of sugar was ATTENUATED due to its high price. At that time, carrots, beets, and other sweet vegetables were mixed together to CONCOCT an ENTICING dessert. The word "carrot," means "orange" in Latin, thus, carrot cake has to be orange, but carrots don't have to be the ingredient responsible for the PIGMENT of the cake. This AESTHETIC dessert, commonly BEDAUBED with frosting, can cause INDIGESTION in the short term and a PROTUBERANT MIDRIFF in the long term.

EPOCH	color
ATTENUATE	create
CONCOCT	tasteful
ENTICE	belly
PIGMENT	reduce
AESTHETIC	bulging
BEDAUB	tempt
INDIGESTION	smear
PROTUBERANT	stomach pain
MIDRIFF	era

Chocolate Cake With Mocha Buttercream
Serves 10

Cake:
1¾ cups flour
2 tsp baking powder
1 tsp baking soda
2 cups sugar
¾ tsp salt
¾ cup unsweetened cocoa
powder
¼ cup semisweet chocolate,
melted
2 tbsp instant coffee powder
½ cup vegetable oil

1 cup whole milk
1 cup warm water
2 eggs
Nonstick cooking spray

Frosting:
2 sticks unsalted butter,
softened to room temperature
1 tbsp unsweetened cocoa
powder
1 tbsp instant coffee powder
½ tsp vanilla extract
1 tbsp milk
1¼ cups powdered sugar
½ cup semisweet chocolate,
melted

Preheat the oven to 350° Fahrenheit.

Grease two 9" round cake pans with the cooking spray, line the bottoms with parchment paper, and grease again.

For the cake: sift together the dry ingredients in a large bowl. In a separate bowl, mix together the wet ingredients, except for the water. Mix the wet into the dry and stir until there are no lumps. Slowly mix in the water. Evenly pour the batter into the cake pans, and bake for about 35 - 40 minutes, or until a toothpick inserted comes out clean. Cool the cakes completely on a cooling rack. Run a knife between each pan and cake and then gently remove each cake from the pan. Set aside while you make the frosting.

For the frosting: whip the butter and vanilla for about 2 minutes in an electric mixer or hand mixer. Add the sugar and continue whipping for about 3 minutes, scraping the bowl as needed. Add the rest of ingredients and keep mixing and scraping until everything is combined.

Frost the top of the first cake. Layer the second cake on top, and frost the top and sides of both cakes to create a frosted, double-layered cake.

Slice and serve.

Mocha cream is my NOMINEE for the OUT-AND-OUT best frosting ever. Add just a MITE of coffee to unsweetened chocolate and be prepared to receive PLAUDITS for a flavor NONPAREIL. ASCETICS may INVEIGH criticism and CITE health concerns but a true SYBARITE can never be held in CHECK.

NOMINEE	pleasure-seeker
OUT-AND-OUT	note
MITE	choice
PLAUDIT	genuinely
NONPAREIL	control
ASCETIC	bit
INVEIGH	praise
CITE	self-denying
SYBARITE	unrivaled
CHECK	utter

Fruit Tart With Graham Cracker Crust
Serves 4 (1 tart per person)

Crust:
8 graham crackers
5 tbsp unsalted butter, melted
1 tbsp sugar

Sweet Cream Filling And Topping:
8 oz softened cream cheese
¼ cup sugar
1 tsp vanilla
2 kiwis
4 strawberries
20 blueberries
12 raspberries
8 blackberries

Preheat the oven to 375° Fahrenheit.

For the crust: in a food processor, pulse the graham crackers, butter, and sugar until the mixture resembles slightly wet sand. Place ¼ of the crust in each of four greased mini tart pans with a removable bottom. Press gently and place in the oven for 10 minutes or until slightly hard to the touch, but not burnt. Remove and let cool.

For the filling: thinly slice the kiwis and strawberries. Combine the cream cheese, sugar, and vanilla. Place ¼ of the mixture in each pan and top with an assortment of the fresh fruit.

Remove each pan bottom, and gently slide a paring knife between the crust and pan. Place each tart on a plate and serve immediately.

*Tip: If there is any sweet cream filling left, place it atop fresh fruit for a sweet dessert.

*Tip: Add small amount of fruit marmalade to make the tart shiny.

In 1829, Sylvester Graham, a Presbyterian minister, promoted the biscuits he invented as part of a dietary REGIMEN designed to STIFLE unhealthy behavior. It remains an ENIGMA as to who deemed it APPROPRIATE to MODIFY the name to "cracker," an ALTERNATIVE whose INADVERTENT consequence was to FACILITATE confusion since "biscuit" more aptly describes a sweet. Graham crackers are now commonly used as snack food and in pie crusts and s'mores, a departure from the original INTENTION that would DISQUIET the good Reverend, if he were alive.

REGIMEN	alter
STIFLE	mystery
ENIGMA	promote
APPROPRIATE	accidental
MODIFY	aim
ALTERNATIVE	upset
INADVERTENT	smother
FACILITATE	acceptable
INTENTION	routine
DISQUIET	option

Orange Cranberry Muffins
Makes 12 - 14 muffins

1 cup dried cranberries
1¼ cups no pulp orange juice
2 cups flour
1 cup sugar
2 tsp baking powder
¼ tsp baking soda
½ tsp salt
1 egg
¼ cup vegetable oil
1 tsp vanilla extract
Nonstick cooking spray

Preheat the oven to 375° Fahrenheit.

Spray a regular size muffin tin with cooking spray and set aside.

Microwave the cranberries and 1 cup of the orange juice on high for about 2 minutes to plump the cranberries. Set aside to cool.

In another bowl, sift the flour, sugar, baking powder, baking soda, and salt. Whisk in the cranberry orange mixture, the extra ¼ cup orange juice, egg, vegetable oil, and vanilla until just combined. Fill each muffin tin about ¾ of the way up.

Bake for about 20 minutes or until a toothpick inserted comes out clean.

Serve.

Muffins are single-serving breads and cakes locked in a COMPETITIVE THRALL with donuts and bagels, VYING for first place among DEVOUT breakfast ENTHUSIASTS. On a sweetness scale, muffins are INTERMEDIATE between the rivals, though not DEFICIENT in calories. This led to the slang, "muffin top," a SARDONIC description of the roll of ABDOMINAL fat that spills over low cut pants, REMINISCENT of the overhang on muffin cups.

COMPETITIVE	religious
THRALL	compete
VIE (VYING)	midway
DEVOUT	fanatic
ENTHUSIAST	sarcastic
INTERMEDIATE	remindful
DEFICIENT	rivalrous
SARDONIC	belly
ABDOMINAL	bondage
REMINISCENT	inadequate

Nutella (Chocolate And Hazelnut) Biscotti
Makes about 25 biscotti

1½ cups flour + more for forming into logs
½ tsp baking powder
½ tsp baking soda
¼ tsp salt
1 tbsp unsweetened cocoa powder
1 egg
⅓ cup sugar
½ cup light brown sugar, lightly packed
½ cup Nutella
1 stick unsalted butter, softened to room temperature
1 tsp vanilla extract
¼ tsp almond extract
¼ cup semisweet chocolate, finely chopped
½ cup hazelnuts, chopped, and toasted + more if you'd like
Nonstick cooking spray

Preheat the oven to 350° Fahrenheit.

Spray a baking sheet with nonstick cooking spray.

Whisk together the egg and sugars until smooth. Set aside.

Combine the flour, baking powder, baking soda, salt, and cocoa powder in a bowl. Whisk together. In another bowl, combine the Nutella, egg and sugars mixture, butter, vanilla extract, and almond extract. Add the dry ingredients and mix well. Stir in the semisweet chocolate and the hazelnuts. Form the dough into two 10" x 2" logs, making sure to flour your hands to prevent sticking, and bake for about 30 - 35 minutes.

Remove from the oven, reduce the temperature of the oven to 300° Fahrenheit, and allow the logs to cool completely. Cut the cooled logs on the bias to achieve long cookies that are about ½" in thickness. Place on the baking sheet and bake on each side for about 10 - 12 minutes.

Let cool completely before serving.

Nutella, a cult favorite consisting of chocolate and hazelnut, was first MANUFACTURED during World War II by Pietro Ferrero, an Italian VENDOR. Chocolate, once BOUNTIFUL, became EXOTIC and SCARCE due to war RATION requirements. Ferrero used hazelnuts, available in PLENTEOUS amounts, as the main ingredient in Nutella. Millions of EXUBERANT fans still ADORE the PROPRIETARY spread.

MANUFACTURE	trademarked
VENDOR	produce
BOUNTIFUL	love
EXOTIC	copious
SCARCE	abundant
RATION	seller
PLENTEOUS	unusual
EXUBERANT	rare
ADORE	enthusiastic
PROPRIETARY	allotment

Nougat
Serves 8 - 12

2 cups sugar
1 cup corn syrup
½ cup honey
¼ cup water
¼ tsp salt
2 egg whites
½ cup toasted whole pistachios (see "White Chocolate Bark" recipe for instructions on toasting nuts)
½ cup toasted whole almonds
1 tbsp orange zest
Nonstick cooking spray

Beat the egg whites using an electric mixer, or by hand, until the eggs hold stiff peaks.

Heat the sugar, water, salt, corn syrup, and honey on a medium - high heat until the sugar dissolves and the mixture reaches 250° Fahrenheit. Whisk ¼ of the mixture into the whipped eggs and continue whipping until the mixture forms stiff peaks. Return the remaining dissolved sugar mixture back to the stove, and cook on a medium - high heat until it reaches 300° Fahrenheit.

With the mixer running (or continue whisking by hand), pour the rest of the hot sugar into the egg whites. Mix until stiff. Fold in the nuts and the zest. Place in a greased loaf pan and spread out completely.

Chill in the refrigerator until the nougat is set. Cut into desired chunks.

Serve.

Nougat candy has an ECCENTRIC NUMERICAL association: its characteristics RECUR in CONSTELLATIONS of three. Its TRIAD of ingredients can be made in TRICOLOR with a choice of TREBLE textures, depending on which of the TRIO of originating countries the nougat is based on. There is one thing that TRANSCENDS all varieties: the TENDENCY of nougat to stick to your teeth!

ECCENTRIC	group
NUMERICAL	threesome
RECUR	set of three
CONSTELLATION	inclination
TRIAD	repeat
TRICOLOR	three
TREBLE	surpass
TRIO	three colors
TRANSCEND	relating to numbers
TENDENCY	bizarre

White Chocolate Bark
Makes 16 pieces

½ cup pistachio nuts
16 oz white chocolate
¼ cup dried cranberries
¼ cup dried apricots
Water

Finely chop the chocolate. Shell and roughly chop the nuts. Thinly slice the apricots.

Toast the pistachios in a medium pan on a medium heat, stirring occasionally for about 3 minutes. You will know when they are done when they start to become golden and give off a nutty smell. Set aside.

Melt the chocolate in a double boiler or place a heatproof bowl over a pot filled halfway with simmering water. Melt the chocolate completely, making sure to continuously stir.

Place a piece of wax paper in an 8" x 10" pan. Pour the melted chocolate in the pan and top with the nuts and dried fruit. Place in the refrigerator for at least 1 hour or until it is completely firm.

Break it into 16 pieces.

Serve.

White "chocolate" is DELINEATED by a misleading MONIKER, because technically it doesn't fit into the category of chocolate. This may seem AMBIGUOUS, but this CONFECTION doesn't NECESSITATE the use of cocoa solids to RENDER it INDESCRIBABLY delicious. In the 1990's, Hershey's chocolate company made white "chocolate" kisses an INDISPENSABLE part of its REPERTOIRE, REVIVING a once loved candy.

DELINEATE	require
MONIKER	collection
AMBIGUOUS	sweet
CONFECTION	characterize
NECESSITATE	name
RENDER	awaken
INDESCRIBABLY	necessary
INDISPENSABLE	inexpressibly
REPERTOIRE	unclear
REVIVE	make

Baklava
Serves 36

Filling:
½ lb unsalted pistachios
½ lb walnuts
¼ cup dried apricots
1 tsp ground cinnamon

2 tbsp honey
16 oz phyllo dough, thawed
per package directions
2 sticks unsalted butter,
melted

Syrup:
1 cup water
½ cup sugar
½ cup honey
Zest of 1 lemon

Preheat the oven to 350° Fahrenheit.

Lightly butter a 9" x 13" baking dish.

For the filling: chop the nuts and apricots into small pieces. Mix together the nuts, apricots, honey, and cinnamon. This works best in a food processor. Set aside.

Place the phyllo on a clean work surface. Measure a piece of phyllo, and if it's bigger than the baking dish, cut it down to fit the dish. Discard the scraps. Make sure to always have a damp cloth covering the stack of phyllo when you aren't using it!

To assemble the baklava, place 1 sheet of phyllo in the dish. Use a pastry brush to lightly butter it all over. Do this 5 more times to form the bottom of the baklava. Spread about ½ cup of the nut mixture onto the baklava base. Place 6 more sheets of phyllo on top, making sure to butter in between, and then another ½ cup of the mixture. Continue this process until you have used all of the nut mixture. Finish with the remaining phyllo pieces, always buttering in between. Cut into about 36 squares and bake for about 40 minutes.

While the baklava is baking, prepare the syrup.

For the syrup: combine the water and sugar in a saucepan and bring the mixture to a boil over a medium - high heat. Add the honey and lemon zest, reduce the heat to low, and reduce the mixture for about 15 minutes, stirring occasionally. As soon as the baklava comes out of the oven, evenly spoon the syrup over each piece.

Cool completely before serving.

The phyllo pastry and chopped nuts in baklava are able to ADHERE to each other because honey is sticky. The action of bees on FLORAL nectars produces honey, a commonly used natural sweetener. Bees RETCH and regurgitate the nectar in REPETITION to make honey. Most honey is now made from bees that are kept in an APIARY. It's IRONIC that we tend to be AMBIVALENT about these winged creatures, PARTICIPATING in their bounty while expressing REPUGNANCE because they are VERMIN.

ADHERE	vomit
FLORAL	bee home
RETCH	uncertain
REPETITION	partake
APIARY	abhorrence
IRONIC	repeatedly
AMBIVALENT	pests
PARTICIPATE	stick
REPUGNANCE	contradictory
VERMIN	flower

Dulce De Leche Pudding
Serves 3

1 (14 oz) can of sweetened condensed milk
1½ cups milk
2 tbsp cornstarch
¼ tsp salt
1 tbsp unsalted butter, softened to room temperature
Water

Remove the paper wrapping from the condensed milk can. Puncture 2 holes on the top of the can to prevent an explosion. Place the can in a small saucepan and fill it up with water, leaving ½" between the water and the top of the can. Bring the water to a simmer, and reduce the heat to low. Let the water simmer for 3½ hours. Make sure to replenish the water, as it will evaporate. Remove the milk can from the pan and allow it to cool completely.

Meanwhile, in a small saucepan on low, bring the milk to a gentle simmer. Add ¾ cup of the condensed milk and the butter and whisk well. Cook it on low until it comes to a light boil, stirring occasionally. Combine the cornstarch and salt in a medium bowl, and add this to the milk mixture. Cook on a medium heat, whisking continuously for 1 minute. Evenly transfer to three ramekins and let cool completely.

Place plastic wrap on top and refrigerate for at least 2 hours.

Serve the extra dulce de leche as a sauce on ice cream or other desserts.

The Maillard reaction is RELEVANT to the MAXIM, "cooking is the EPITOME of chemistry." It describes the browning that results as sugar and an amino acid INTERACT. Dulce de leche depends on the Maillard reaction and caramelization occurring in UNISON, both requiring heat as a PROMOTER of the process. Thank chemistry for the MELLIFLUOUS texture and REDOLENT aroma that make this dessert a favorite. It would be REMISS not to recognize Louis-Camille Maillard, the scientist at the GENESIS of our enjoyment, for his wonderful contribution.

RELEVANT	adage
MAXIM	encourager
EPITOME	negligent
INTERACT	creation
UNISON	fragrant
PROMOTER	accord
MELLIFLUOUS	mix
REDOLENT	essence
REMISS	flowing
GENESIS	applicable

Orange Tea Infused Hot Chocolate
Serves 2 - 3

¼ cup boiling hot water
2 orange tea bags
¼ cup sugar
3½ tbsp unsweetened cocoa powder
2 cups milk

Steep the tea bags in the hot water for about 3 minutes. Remove the bags.

Combine the steeped water, sugar, and cocoa powder in a pot. Stir and cook on a medium heat for about 3 minutes. Add the milk and cook for another 5 minutes, stirring occasionally, or until the milk is warm.

Serve.

Hot chocolate, in its RUDIMENTARY form, was QUITE different from the GRANULAR, packed powder found in most supermarkets today. It dates back to 460 A.D., and now, Mayan hieroglyphs provide clues as to the way in which the drink was served, often in LUXURIOUS METAL pots. No VESTIGES of these ARCHAIC vessels remain. The INDIGENOUS Mayan drink quickly grew in popularity, was MODERNIZED in Europe and eventually MIGRATED to America.

RUDIMENTARY	fully
QUITE	roam
GRANULAR	improve
LUXURIOUS	native
METAL	basic
VESTIGE	ancient
ARCHAIC	chemical element
INDIGENOUS	particulate
MODERNIZE	extravagant
MIGRATE	remnant

Ginger Scones
Makes 12 medium (2" - 3") scones

3 cups flour + more for shaping
¾ cup minced candied ginger
1½ tbsp grated ginger root
¾ cup sugar
¾ cup buttermilk
10 tbsp unsalted butter, melted
¼ tsp salt
1 tsp baking soda
¾ tsp baking powder
1 tsp vanilla extract
Nonstick cooking spray

Preheat the oven to 400° Fahrenheit.

Spray a large sheet pan with nonstick cooking spray.

In a large bowl, sift together the dry ingredients. Add both the candied and fresh ginger, and mix. Pour in the butter, buttermilk and vanilla, and mix until just combined. Divide the dough into 2 balls.

Lightly flour a surface. Shape or roll each of the balls into circles that are about 1" thick. Cut each into 6 wedges and place on the prepared baking pan. Bake for about 18 minutes.

Cool for 10 minutes before serving.

*Tip: To make a glaze for the scones, combine 1 cup powdered sugar and 2 tbsp milk. Pour over the scones immediately after they come out of the oven. Let the glaze harden completely before serving.

Ginger is at the root of "Gingervitis," a CONTRIVED HEREDITARY disease featured in a South Park EPISODE. If you have ever been told to steer clear of "Ginger Kids," just CHORTLE at this IRRATIONAL BABBLE, a bunch of HUMBUG. Ginger root can be DILUTED with water to extract medicinal value or give food a PIQUANT touch, which if overdone, can become INCENDIARY.

CONTRIVED	segment
HEREDITARY	fiery
EPISODE	nonsense
CHORTLE	inherited
IRRATIONAL	attenuate
BABBLE	laugh
HUMBUG	flavorful
DILUTE	phony
PIQUANT	absurd
INCENDIARY	chatter

Cinnamon Rolls
Serves 20

Rolls:
1 loaf frozen bread dough, defrosted
1 stick melted unsalted butter + more for the dish
¾ cup brown sugar, packed
2 tbsp ground cinnamon
½ tsp nutmeg
¼ cup raisins, optional
¼ cup chopped nuts, optional

Frosting:
8 oz cream cheese, softened
3 tbsp unsalted butter, softened
¾ cup powdered sugar
¾ tsp vanilla extract

Preheat the oven to 350° Fahrenheit.

Butter 1 or 2 cake pans.

For the rolls: roll out the dough to an 18" x 6" rectangle. Mix together the melted butter, sugar, cinnamon, nutmeg, raisins and nuts. Spread the mixture all over the dough. Roll it up, starting from one long edge, in a jellyroll fashion. Cut 20 slices and place them cut side down in a baking dish. Let the rolls rise for about 1 hour. Place them in the oven and bake for about 25 minutes.

For the frosting: whisk together the frosting ingredients, and immediately pour over the rolls after they come out of the oven.

Cool completely before serving.

It might seem that only the WITLESS would consume tree bark, but to be ACCURATE, that's the OPERATIVE action when we eat cinnamon. It sounds WRETCHED, but that RENDITION of the truth doesn't ATTEST to the delicious taste and pleasing AROMA of this spice. Those in the know MARVEL at its health benefits, a BENISON in disguise, and ignore those who choose to DISPARAGE it.

WITLESS	disgusting
ACCURATE	foolish
OPERATIVE	affirm
WRETCHED	be amazed
RENDITION	correct
ATTEST	criticize
AROMA	version
MARVEL	functioning
BENISON	smell
DISPARAGE	blessing

Shortbread Cookies Dipped In Chocolate
Makes about 20 cookies

Cookies:
¼ cup sugar
¼ tsp salt
1 cup all-purpose flour + more for rolling
1 stick unsalted butter, softened to room temperature

Chocolate Dip:
4 oz semisweet chocolate
Water

Preheat the oven to 350° Fahrenheit.

Line two baking sheets with parchment paper.

To make the cookies: cream the butter and sugar until light and fluffy, using a hand mixer, stand mixer, or by hand. Pour in the flour and salt and blend until combined. Turn out the dough onto a floured surface and roll until the dough is about ¼" thick. Use about a 1½" cookie cutter to make the cookies. Place on the prepared pans and bake for about 8 - 10 minutes or until the cookies are lightly golden around the edges. Let them cool completely on a wire rack.

To make the chocolate dip: finely chop the chocolate. Use a double boiler or a heatproof bowl set over a pot filled halfway with simmering water, and place the chocolate in the bowl. Stir continuously for a few minutes or until the chocolate is melted.

Dip the cookies halfway in the chocolate and place them on a pan lined with parchment paper until the chocolate completely hardens.

Serve.

CREDIBLE sources attribute the origin of shortbread to the 16th century ICON, Mary, Queen of Scots. The REQUISITE feature of this UNLEAVENED biscuit is its texture. "BRITTLE" and "crumbly" are ANTIQUATED definitions of "short," ergo the name. By EXTENSION, "shortening" refers to any fat used to INSTILL a flaky texture. To DECORATE, puncture, but do not PERFORATE, the surface of the cookies, then cut them into hearts, fingers, and other interesting shapes.

CREDIBLE	penetrate
ICON	infuse
REQUISITE	fragile
UNLEAVENED	stretching
BRITTLE	necessary
ANTIQUATED	embellish
EXTENSION	likeness
INSTILL	old
DECORATE	unraised
PERFORATE	believable

Chocolate Chip Cookies
Makes about 44 cookies

1 stick softened unsalted butter
½ cup vegetable oil
¾ cup granulated sugar
¾ cup packed brown sugar
2 eggs
2½ cups flour
1 tsp baking soda
¼ tsp baking powder
¼ tsp salt
1½ - 2 cups semisweet chocolate chips

Preheat the oven to 375° Fahrenheit.

In a stand mixer, cream the butter, oil and both sugars. Add the eggs one at a time. Slowly mix in all of the dry ingredients. Remove from the stand mixer and add in the desired amount of chocolate chips and stir with a spatula.

Place a sheet of wax paper on a sheet pan and scoop 1 - 2 tbsp of batter on the wax paper, leaving 2 inches between each cookie.

Bake for 10 - 14 minutes or until the edges are golden and the center is soft.

Cool completely before serving.

Chocolate chip cookies, sometimes known by their ALIAS, "choco" chip cookies, can be RELISHED in a variety of forms including cookies, ice cream, sandwiches, bars, and squares. Any cookie FANATIC would enjoy the history of their origin. It started in 1937, when the owner and chef of The Toll House Inn, a lodging spot for WEARISOME travelers, Ruth Graves Wakefield, decided to ALTER her butter cookie recipe by adding semisweet chocolate, which became an INSTANT hit. The word about Ruth's recipe spread RAPIDLY, WHEREUPON the UBIQUITOUS chocolate company, Nestlé, offered to print her recipe on each chocolate chip package and a give her a lifetime supply of chocolate. Ruth's recipe has inspired cooks, and the baking of her cookies has become an American PASTIME.

ALIAS	omnipresent
RELISH	zealot
FANATIC	hobby
WEARISOME	immediate
ALTER	after which
INSTANT	adjust
RAPIDLY	savor
WHEREUPON	pseudonym
UBIQUITOUS	tired
PASTIME	quickly

Molasses Cookies
Makes 30 cookies

2¼ cups flour
¼ cup white sugar
1¼ cup lightly packed brown sugar
¾ cup unsalted butter, melted
1 egg
¼ cup molasses
2 tsp baking soda
¼ tsp baking powder
1 tsp ground cinnamon
½ tsp ground ginger
¼ tsp salt
Nonstick cooking spray

Preheat the oven to 375° Fahrenheit.

Grease a baking sheet with the spray. You may need to use more than one baking sheet.

Combine the butter and both sugars in a bowl. Whisk in the egg and molasses, then add all of the other ingredients. Cover the bowl with plastic wrap and refrigerate for one hour.

When you are ready to bake, take about 1 tbsp of the cookie dough and roll it into a ball. Repeat this process and place each of the cookies 2" apart on the baking sheet.

Bake for about 10 - 13 minutes and then let cool completely.

Serve.

*Tip: Before baking, roll the cookie dough balls in a ½ cup of white sugar.

Molasses may be SALUTARY for your health, but it's not completely INNOCUOUS. In 1919, a storage tank filled with molasses SPONTANEOUSLY burst, unleashing two million gallons of sweet syrup that UNDULATED through town at high speed. IMMENSE waves UPROOTED buildings and WRESTED a bridge from its base, WREAKING HAVOC along its path. The DELUGE, known as the "Boston Molasses Disaster," was responsible for 21 deaths and many more injuries.

SALUTARY	huge
INNOCUOUS	flood
SPONTANEOUSLY	chaotic
UNDULATE	cause
IMMENSE	beneficial
UPROOT	flow
WREST	displace
WREAK	harmless
HAVOC	pulled
DELUGE	automatically

Apple Rhubarb Sauce
Serves 6

6 small apples, any kind (about 8 cups when chopped)
3 large stalks rhubarb (about 3 cups when chopped)
½ cup orange juice
½ cup apple juice
½ cup water
1 tsp cinnamon
½ tsp nutmeg
2 tbsp granulated sugar + extra to taste
2 tsp vanilla extract

Peel and core the apples and chop them into bite size pieces. Chop the rhubarb into bite size pieces.

Combine all of the ingredients in a large pot. Mix, cover, and cook on a low heat for 30 minutes, stirring occasionally until the apples and rhubarb are soft.

Add the mixture to a food processor or blender and pulse until the sauce has reached your desired texture. Let cool, then refrigerate.

Serve at desired temperature.

Rhubarb is unusual in that its BOTANICAL description was ENJOINED in 1947 in a New York court. There, the DETERMINATION was made that rhubarb is a fruit, thus defying the CONSENSUS among plant experts, who up until then had CLASSIFIED it as a vegetable. The ruling was a clever STRATAGEM designed to PREEMPT those who sought to LEVY a high tax on this popular produce. Rhubarb has a tart flavor and is SUFFUSED with a rich, red color that adds ALLURE to any presentation.

BOTANICAL	trick
ENJOIN	categorize
DETERMINATION	command
CONSENSUS	cover
CLASSIFY	plant related
STRATAGEM	agreement
PREEMPT	collect
LEVY	appeal
SUFFUSE	prevent
ALLURE	settlement

Fruit Parfait
Serves 1 - 2

½ cup vanilla yogurt
1 apricot
2 large strawberries
20 blueberries
10 raspberries
1 biscotti (any type)
2 tbsp coconut flakes

Thinly slice the apricot and strawberries. Crush the biscotti.

Place ¼ cup of yogurt on the bottom of a tall glass.

Place ½ of the biscotti, ½ of the apricot, the slices of 1 strawberry, 10 blueberries, 5 raspberries and 1 tbsp of the coconut flakes over the yogurt.

Layer the rest of the yogurt, coconut and the remaining fruit and biscotti on top.

Serve.

In French, "parfait" means "perfect." The term no longer EXCLUSIVELY describes a frozen dessert, having EVOLVED over time to a much more COMPREHENSIVE meaning. Any dish stacked with contrasting STRATA of food served in a tall, TRANSPARENT glass can LEGITIMATELY be called "parfait." Let your imagination MEANDER but be mindful of the need for an ESTHETIC presentation as you VISUALIZE the creative OPTIONS.

———

EXCLUSIVELY	envision
EVOLVE	layers
COMPREHENSIVE	choice
STRATA	wander
TRANSPARENT	inclusive
LEGITIMATE	clear
MEANDER	rightful
ESTHETIC	solely
VISUALIZE	develop
OPTION	pleasing

Poached Pears
Serves 4

4 Bosc pears, slightly ripe
3½ cups water
½ cup grape juice
1¼ cups sugar
1 tsp vanilla extract

Peel and core the pears and cut into quarters.

In a large saucepan, heat the water, juice, sugar, and vanilla on a medium – low heat until all of the sugar is dissolved. Place the pears in the liquid and cook on low for about 20 minutes. Turn off the heat and let the pears and the liquid cool until they reach room temperature.

Serve the pear slices with a spoonful of the sauce.

*Tip: For an exotic twist, use açai or pomegranate juice instead of grape juice.

The DECIDUOUS pear, a delicious fruit related to the apple, is representative of POISE and beauty, but is also notorious for inauspicious reasons. The overwhelming PLURALITY of pears have trouble FORFENDING attacks by ARRANT NEFARIOUS pests, and therefore suffer from numerous AILMENTS. Affected trees are less RAMOSE and the fruit they bear is PALY in appearance and loses its AIRY texture.

———

DECIDUOUS	dull
POISE	variety
PLURALITY	disease
FORFEND	delicate
ARRANT	gracefulness
NEFARIOUS	downright
AILMENT	having branches
RAMOSE	sheds leaves annually
PALY	prevent
AIRY	foul

Grilled Peaches With Vanilla Mascarpone
Serves 4

2 ripe peaches
⅓ cup mascarpone cheese, softened
1½ tbsp powdered sugar
1 tsp vanilla extract
Canola or vegetable oil

Cut the peaches in half and seed.

Preheat a grill or a grill pan to a medium - high heat.

Lightly drizzle the pan with the vegetable or canola oil.

Place the peaches on the pan and grill for about 2 - 3 minutes on each side. While they are cooking, combine the mascarpone, powdered sugar and vanilla in a bowl.

Once the peaches are cooked, dollop the mascarpone on each peach.

Serve.

Feeling LETHARGIC after a TOILSOME day in the kitchen? Seeking the ESSENCE of simplicity, an EMBLEM of the divine? Grilled peaches offer a PEERLESS FINALE to an otherwise INTRICATE meal. This SUCCULENT and sweet AMBROSIA will delight the most DISCRIMINATING palate. Easy meets impressive in this dessert!

LETHARGIC	laborious
TOILSOME	complicated
ESSENCE	selective
EMBLEM	spirit
PEERLESS	mouth-watering
FINALE	unrivaled
INTRICATE	lazy
SUCCULENT	pleasing to taste
AMBROSIA	symbol
DISCRIMINATING	end

Gourmet Banana Split Sundae
Serves 1 - 2

1 ripe banana
3 scoops ice cream
1 tbsp milk
2 tbsp chocolate chips, milk or semisweet
1 tbsp dulce de leche (see dulce de leche pudding recipe)
3 marshmallows
1 tbsp shredded coconut flakes

Slice the banana in half lengthwise and place the two slices on a plate. Align the ice cream scoops in a row over the banana slices.

For the chocolate sauce: melt the milk and chocolate chips in the microwave until a completely smooth mixture forms. Drizzle the chocolate sauce and dulce de leche sauce on the ice cream.

Skewer the marshmallows on a wooden kabob stick. Toast them over a medium flame until golden. Be sure to constantly rotate the stick to prevent burning. Toasting works best if you have a gas burning stove.

For the toasted coconut: place the shreds in a small pan and cook them on a medium heat, stirring occasionally until they start to become golden. This should only take a few minutes. Sprinkle the coconut on top of the sauces.

Serve.

*Tip: For extra decadence, top with whipped cream and crushed nuts.

There is a simple solution if waiting a FORTNIGHT for fruit to ripen is an INTOLERABLE delay that will THWART and BELATE your meal plan. Place the fruit in a brown paper bag to PROMPT the production of ethylene gas, which causes softening. MOLLYCODDLE the fruit and be COGNIZANT of the ripening process because the transition from solid to mush can occur PRECIPITOUSLY. The quote, "If one apple is TAINTED, it will MAR the whole bunch," is a reminder to avoid putting bruised fruit in the bag.

FORTNIGHT	spoil
INTOLERABLE	aware
THWART	blemished
BELATE	pamper
PROMPT	insufferable
MOLLYCODDLE	abrupt
COGNIZANT	delay
PRECIPITOUS	initiate
TAINTED	prevail
MAR	two weeks

From The Back Cover

"Cook Your Way Through The S.A.T." is a DELECTABLE way to master frequently-asked SAT vocabulary. Serve your RAVENOUS appetite for learning with this INNOVATIVE book. Each of the 99 easy, enjoyable recipes is matched with a fun-fact blurb containing 10 SAT words. Wondering why onions STIMULATE the LACHRYMAL glands or how Gorgonzola cheese ACQUIRES its blue color? Memorizing SAT vocabulary doesn't have to be an ARDUOUS task. Retain 1000 words while SIMULTANEOUSLY becoming an ADEPT chef. This book is a great tool for ASSUAGING those pre-SAT fears.

DELECTABLE	formidable
RAVENOUS	skilled
INNOVATIVE	delightful
STIMULATE	concurrent
LACHRYMAL	activate
ACQUIRE	tear
ARDUOUS	insatiable
SIMULTANEOUS	original
ADEPT	relieve
ASSUAGE	obtain

Index Of Vocabulary By Recipe

Fennel And Pear Salad

mythologic · legendary
utilize · use
loot ·plunder
dispense· ·provide
mundane ·worldly
bulbous· round
akin· similar
albeit· ·although
ingredient · · · · · · · · · · · · · · · · · component
revile· abuse

Chop Chop Salad

etymology · · · · · · · · · · · · · · · · · ·word history
accelerate· quicken
haste · rush
hew · cut
conjoin ·unite
connotation · · · · · · · · · · · · · · · · · meaning
pithy · concise
galvanize· · · · · · · · · · · · · · · · · · · animate
impious· · · · · · · · · · · · · · · · · · ·disrespectful
admonish· warn

Greek Salad

monotone · · · · · · · · · · · · · · · · · ·sameness
rustic· rural
disparate · · · · · · · · · · · · · · · · · · unequal
unify ·unite
scintillate · · · · · · · · · · · · · · · · · · spark
predominant · · · · · · · · · · · · · · · ·overriding
brine ·saltwater
medial · middle
spectrum · · · · · · · · · · · · · · · · · · range
preference · · · · · · · · · · · · · · · · · ·choice

Watermelon, Feta, and Tomato Salad

proffer · offer
conjecture · guess
delicacy · fine food
appellation · name
prevarication · · · · · · · · · · · · · · · · · · deception
edible ·consumable
purveyor · supplier
originated · began
nutritive · nourishing
longevity · resilience

Lima Bean And Cilantro Salad

confederacy ·league
irrepressible · · · · · · · · · · · · · · · uncontrollable
odium · dislike
plebian ·common
vilify · slander
chastise · · · · · · · · · · · · · · · · · · · criticize
venom ·poison
harangue · · · · · · · · · · · · · · · · · · ·criticism
candor ·honesty
inexhaustible · · · · · · · · · · · · · · · · ·unlimited

Black Bean And Corn Salad

denizen ·inhabitant
vocation · job
robust ·powerful
diverse · various
species · group
ashen · pale
alabaster · · · · · · · · · · · · · · · · · · · white
tint · hue
burgeon ·grow
cereal ·grain

Wedge Salad

domestic · household
tranquility · calm
imbroglio · · · · · · · · · · · · · · · · · · entanglement
simplify · make easier
impel · drive
palpable · tangible
trammel · · · · · · · · · · · · · · · · · · · impediment
impede · hinder
rationalism · reason
weal · well-being

Fig And Olive Tapenade On Baked Baguette

whet · stimulate
initiate · begin
fundamental · · · · · · · · · · · · · · · · · · · basic
component · part
tantalize · excite
propel · push
palate · appetite
trajectory · path
prosaic · · · · · · · · · · · · · · · · commonplace
coerce · bully

Smoked Salmon, Cucumber, And Cream Cheese On Baguette

iconoclast · rebel
fusion · mixture
appall · shock
disregard · · · · · · · · · · · · · · · · · · · neglect
fealty · loyalty
substantive · · · · · · · · · · · · · · · · · · solid
sylph · · · · · · · · · · · · · · · · · · slender being
dauntless · · · · · · · · · · · · · · · · · · fearless
loathe · hate
gratify · satisfy

Pea Prosciutto Soup

preservation · conservation
typical · normal
subjected · · · · · · · · · · · · · · · · · · · put through
rancid · rotten
beneficial · useful
reproduce · breed
tinge · tint
desiccate · dry
prolong ·lengthen
gourmand · · · · · · · · · · · · · · · · · · ·connoisseur

Potage Parmentier (Potato Leek Soup)

expatriate ·emigrant
adroit · skillful
testament · evidence
commentary · · · · · · · · · · · · · · · · ·explanation
technique ·method
insight · · · · · · · · · · · · · · · · · ·perceptiveness
mimic · imitate
tantamount · · · · · · · · · · · · · · · · ·equivalent
aspire ·aim
iota · speck

Corn Chowder

prodigious ·immense
allude · refer
maize · corn
propagate ·spread
acreage · land
kernel · nugget
practicable · · · · · · · · · · · · · · · · · · ·feasible
ponderous · · · · · · · · · · · · · · · · · · weighty
tangible · · · · · · · · · · · · · · · · · · · touchable
hazard · danger

Chicken And Dumpling Soup

regalia · royal emblems
abundant · plentiful
penury · poverty
subsistence · survival
solvent · debt-free
well-to-do · · · · · · · · · · · · · · · · · · · prosperous
reunite · rejoin
adieu · goodbye
significant · important
success · · · · · · · · · · · · · · · · · · · accomplishment

Gazpacho

ascribe · attribute
bibulous · · · · · · · · · · · · · · · · · · fond of drinking
aqueous · water
cornucopia · · · · · · · · · · · · · · · · · · abundance
enormous · huge
masterpiece · · · · · · · · · · · · · outstanding work
discovery · finding
embody · manifest
belittle · denigrate
excusable · · · · · · · · · · · · · · · · · · · pardonable

Brussels Sprouts And Mushroom Tart

bevy · cluster
antiquity · past
nondescript · · · · · · · · · · · · · · · · indescribable
dire · dreadful
onus · burden
deleterious · · · · · · · · · · · · · · · · · · · harmful
vigilant · alert
knotty · complicated
prudent · cautious
eclectic · diverse

Pear And Gorgonzola Tart

noxious · unpleasant
intimidate · frighten
intrepid · fearless
aversion · dislike
balk · refuse
derive ·obtain
variegated · · · · · · · · · · · · · · · · · ·different
savory · tangy
tempered · · · · · · · · · · · · · · · · · · neutralized
palatable ·tasty

Sylvia's Steamed Cabbage, Coriander And Ground Meat

vernacular · · · · · · · · · · · · · everyday language
resource · supply
confer · grant
buffoon · clown
inane ·stupid
vapid · dull
aspersion · · · · · · · · · · · · · · · · · · · slander
execrable · · · · · · · · · · · · · · · · · ·abominable
mockery ·ridicule
sagacious · · · · · · · · · · · · · · · · · · · wise

Nancy's Hummus With Pita Chips

lobbyist · · · · · · · · · person influencing legislators
characterize · · · · · · · · · · · · · · · · · · describe
unique · · · · · · · · · · · · · · · · · · ·one of a kind
rancor · · · · · · · · · · · · · · · · · · · bitterness
provocative · · · · · · · · · · · · · · · ·stimulating
contravene · · · · · · · · · · · · · · · · · obstruct
exemplary · · · · · · · · · · · · · · · · · a model
wary · cautious
discredit · · · · · · · · · · · · · · · · · ·dishonor
substantiate · · · · · · · · · · · · · · · · ·validate

Onion Casserole

equanimity · · · · · · · · · · · · · · · · · · · composure
stimulus · · · · · · · · · · · · · · · · · · · inspiration
grief · distress
apparent ·obvious
volatile · unstable
irritant ·annoyance
unavoidable · · · · · · · · · · · · · · · · · inevitable
submerge· sink
depress · lower
quiescent ·inactive

Latkes (Potato Pancakes)

fête · celebration
integrity · · · · · · · · · · · · · · · · · · wholeness
knead · massage
resemble · · · · · · · · · · · · · · · · · · ·parallel
deviate· ·diverge
commemorate · · · · · · · · · · · · · · · · · honor
predicament · · · · · · · · · · · · · · · · · ·plight
salvage· save
minute · trifling
captivate · · · · · · · · · · · · · · · · · · enrapture

Steamed Bok Choy With Collard Greens

dissimilar · · · · · · · · · · · · · · · · · ·different
tremendous · · · · · · · · · · · · · · · · · ·wonderful
neuter ·sexless
delectation· · · · · · · · · · · · · · · · · · delight
concord ·harmony
afire· burning
ablution· · · · · · · · · · · · · · · · · · · washing
drowsy· ·sleepy
superficial · · · · · · · · · · · · · · · · · · surface
disinfect ·clean

Fried Green Tomatoes

prototype· ·model
comical · funny
folklore · tales
embolden · encourage
eatable· ·palatable
generally · mainly
florid · red
generate· produce
exceed · surpass
gladden · delight

Roasted Red Peppers

nomadic · wandering
memento· souvenir
eminent· respected
refer· mention
renown · fame
affluent ·wealthy
confound · confuse
nomenclature· · · · · · · · · · · · · · · · · · · name
cultivate ·grow
myriad· many

Spicy Stewed Potatoes

excess ·superfluous
quarter ·one fourth
populace · · · · · · · · · · · · · · · · · · inhabitants
emigrate · resettle
quintessential · · · · · · · · · · · · · · · · · typical
assailant· attacker
disseminate · · · · · · · · · · · · · · · · · ·spread
ultimately · · · · · · · · · · · · · · · · · · ·finally
eradicate · · · · · · · · · · · · · · · · · · · destroy
annihilation· · · · · · · · · · · · · · · · · destruction

Glazed Carrots

riddance · · · · · · · · · · · · · · · · · deliverance from
rigmarole· ·nonsense
serviceable· ·usable
courageous· brave
demeanor· · · · · · · · · · · · · · · · · · · conduct
mendacious · · · · · · · · · · · · · · · · · untrue
dexterity · · · · · · · · · · · · · · · · · · · skill
composure ·calm
severe · intense
cosmetic · · · · · · · · · · · · · · · · · · · external

Asparagus With Hollandaise Sauce

acclaim · praise
tepid · warm
lustrous ·shining
croissant · · · · · · · · · · · · · · French butter roll
artisan · · · · · · · · · · · · · · · · · craftsperson
kin ·relation
lowly· ·humble
unbecoming · · · · · · · · · · · · · · · unattractive
laxative · · · · · · · · · · · · · · · bowel stimulant
noisome· · · · · · · · · · · · · · · · · · ·malodorous

Brown Rice With Almonds And Raisins

pudgy · plump
auburn· tawny
uppermost· · · · · · · · · · · · · · · · · · · ·outer
scythe ·tool
supernumerary· · · · · · · · · · · · · · · · ·excessive
titanic ·huge
plenitude· · · · · · · · · · · · · · · · · abundance
flux · change
refuse· decline
perhaps ·maybe

Fried Plantains

entirety · whole
parentage · origin
finite · limited
allotment · portion
differentiate · · · · · · · · · · · · · · · · · · discriminate
inadvisable · unwise
proportionate · · · · · · · · · · · · · · · · corresponding
operate · act
noticeable · · · · · · · · · · · · · · · · · · · conspicuous
mandatory · required

Roasted Butternut Squash With Dried Cranberries

figurative · symbolic
revere · admire
jovial · friendly
badger · pester
cloying · overly sweet
flamboyant · · · · · · · · · · · · · · · · · · · theatrical
exaggerate · · · · · · · · · · · · · · · · · · · embellish
outlandish · zany
ribald · vulgar
gaiety · festivity

Rosemary And Thyme Scalloped Potatoes

hale · healthy
stigma · flaw
indulgence · luxury
suppress · restrain
proscribe · ban
criterion · standard
velvety · soft
recapitulate · repeat
retention · holding
estimable · · · · · · · · · · · · · · · · · · appreciable

Pork Buns

recognized · identified
extraordinary · · · · · · · · · · · · · · · · · · · remarkable
commodity ·product
formula ·method
cartilage · · · · · · · · · · · · · · · · · ·connective tissue
basting · · · · · · · · · · · · · · · · · · ·pouring juices
leaven · raise
ladling· ·spooning
accomplish · · · · · · · · · · · · · · · · · · · achieve
enrapture· delight

Vegetable Kabobs

sequence ·order
existence · being
intellect· mind
inventive· · · · · · · · · · · · · · · · · · · ·creative
analogous · · · · · · · · · · · · · · · · · · ·comparable
inadequate· · · · · · · · · · · · · · · · · · · lacking
aperture· opening
sufficient · · · · · · · · · · · · · · · · · · ·adequate
discernible· · · · · · · · · · · · · · · · · · recognizable
incinerate · · · · · · · · · · · · · · ·destroy by burning

Scallops Gratin

feminine · · · · · · · · · · · · · · · · · · · woman-like
visual· perceptible
protective · · · · · · · · · · · · · · · · · · · shielding
nurture · foster
principle · idea
sisterhood · · · · · · · · · · · · · ·female association
pagan · · · · · · · · · · · · · · · · · · ·non-Christian
theology ·religion
solar · sun-related
terminate· ·end

Margherita Panini (Tomato, Basil and Mozzarella Panini)

triumvirate · threesome
venerate · honor
recollect · recall
grandiloquent ·pompous
consort · companion
encompass ·include
appreciably · · · · · · · · · · · · · · · · · ·considerably
variation · · · · · · · · · · · · · · · · · · ·modification
compress ·flatten
peerage · nobility

Fish In Parchment

tyro ·beginner
hone ·sharpen
nascent · budding
extol · praise
prowess · skill
literally · objectively
tumescent ·swollen
waft · float
titillate · stimulate
olfactory · · · · · · · · · · · · · · · ·relating to smell

Mushroom Risotto

guess ·surmise
nimble · quick
nonchalant · · · · · · · · · · · · · · · · · · · indifferent
perspicacious · · · · · · · · · · · · · · · · · ·astute
vex · irritate
notorious ·infamous
haggard ·worn
gusto · enjoyment
invaluable · · · · · · · · · · · · · · · · · · · precious
perquisite · · · · · · · · · · · · · · · · · · · benefit

Meat Lasagna

fictitious · fabricated
abstemious · restrained
oblong · elongated
telltale · giveaway
obesity · · · · · · · · · · · · being grossly overweight
distensible · stretchable
flagrant · conspicuous
leonine · lion-like
obstreperous · · · · · · · · · · · · · · · · · · · boisterous
wane · decrease

Cheese Cannelloni

erroneous · incorrect
Milky Way · galaxy
creamy · buttery
forté · talent
decorate · adorn
outdo · beat
betrothed · engaged
ministry · prayer
osculate · kiss
bliss · ecstasy

Pesto Pizza

transient · impermanent
acerbic · bitter
hypothesis · theory
sinister · evil
implicate · involve
counterfeit · fake
inedible · uneatable
utmost · greatest
spurious · phony
subvert · undermine

Tortellini with White Cream Sauce and Artichokes

apology · explanation
anxious · concerned
arbitrary · · · · · · · · · · · · · · · · · · · unpredictable
debatable · disputable
intuition · · · · · · · · · · · · · · · · · · · intuitiveness
naturally · innately
vincible · conquerable
fortitude · bravery
forgo · sacrifice
aliment · food

Baked Macaroni

pretentious · snobbish
patronizing · · · · · · · · · · · · · · · · · · · frequenting
convenience · · · · · · · · · · · · · · · · · accessibility
patrician · aristocrat
satiate · satisfy
fervent · enthusiastic
festive · celebratory
slightly · somewhat
ostentatious · flashy
fidelity · faithfulness

Rotini Primavera

monotonous · dull
infinite · limitless
encyclopedia · · · · · · · · · · · comprehensive book
linear · straight
convex · · · · · · · · · curving as the surface of a circle
cycloid · like a circle
spheroid · sphere-like
circumference · · · · · · · · · · · · · · · · · · perimeter
gyrate · rotate
corporeal · bodily

Eggplant Parmesan

vegetarian · meatless
sustenance · food
accommodate · · · · · · · · · · · · · · · · · · help
carnivorous · · · · · · · · · · · · · · · · · meat lover
augment · increase
quantity · amount
protract · prolong
eventual · ultimate
intensive · · · · · · · · · · · · · · · · · · exhaustive
irresistible · · · · · · · · · · · · · · · · · · tempting

Ratatouille

homonym · · · · · · · same sound/different meaning
quixotic · idealistic
penchant · liking
fastidious · · · · · · · · · · · · · · · · · · meticulous
repository · · · · · · · · · · · · · · · · · storage place
animate · enliven
revise · modify
detrimental · · · · · · · · · · · · · · · · · injurious
dutiful · devoted
productive · · · · · · · · · · · · · · · · · · prolific

Cheese Soufflé

surmount · · · · · · · · · · · · · · · · · · · overcome
imperative · · · · · · · · · · · · · · · · · · necessary
subtrahend · · · · · · · · · · · · · · · · · · subtract
safeguard · · · · · · · · · · · · · · · · · · · protect
translucent · · · · · · · · · · · · · semitransparent
agglomerate · · · · · · · · · · · · · · · · · aggregate
undermine · · · · · · · · · · · · · · · · · · weaken
imperil · jeopardize
perseverance · · · · · · · · · · · · · · · · · dedication
proficiency · · · · · · · · · · · · · · · · · · · skill

Meal In A Pita Pocket

plausible · possible
instance · case
sheer · utter
promulgate · proclaim
observant · watchful
influx · flow
expand · enlarge
explosive · increasing
precaution · safeguard
ardor · enthusiasm

Lemon Shrimp With Garlic Sauce

clarified · clear
facile · easy
meditation · · · · · · · · · · · · · · · contemplation
purl · stir
ready · prepared
cessation · end
progression · · · · · · · · · · · · · · · · · movement
bitterness · · · · · · · · · · · · · · · · · · · harshness
extraneous · · · · · · · · · · · · · · · · · superfluous
opaque · cloudy

Braised Short Ribs

transition · passage
sear · char
avant-garde · · · · · · · · · · · · · · · · cutting edge
infuse · introduce
frugal · economical
sumptuous · rich
inexpensive · · · · · · · · · · · · · · · · · low-priced
variable · changing
contingent · · · · · · · · · · · · · · · · · conditional
pusillanimous · · · · · · · · · · · · · · · · · · timid

Roasted Lemon Chicken With Pine Nut Couscous

travail · struggle

phenomenal· · · · · · · · · · · · · · · · · · · exceptional

absorbing · consuming

progressively · · · · · · · · · · · · · · · · · · gradually

diminutive · tiny

prerogative ·right

expedient· ·hasty

abbreviate · shorten

dominate ·rule

prosperity · wealth

Mediterranean Turkey Meatloaf

bask· lounge

radiance· sparkle

dehydrate ·dry out

necessary · · · · · · · · · · · · · · · · · · indispensable

perceptible · · · · · · · · · · · · · · · · · recognizable

shrinkage· · · · · · · · · · · · · · · · · · · contraction

shrivel ·wrinkle

deplete · lessen

benefit· ·advantage

vitality ·zest

Fish Cakes

glimpse · look

topography · · · · · · · · · · · · · physical features

decisive ·definite

domain ·area

inhospitable· · · · · · · · · · · · · · · unwelcoming

predictably · · · · · · · · · · · · · can be foretold

discard· reject

habitant· · · · · · · · · · · · · · · · · · · ·denizen

adjacent· · · · · · · · · · · · · · · · · · · adjoining

estuary· · · · · · · · · · · · · narrow body of water

Fried Rice

miscellany · mixture
ocular · visual
sensation · knockout
tailor · fit
liking · preference
cull · select
efficient · organized
impersonal · · · · · · · · · · · · · · · · · · inattentive
service · assistance
penultimate · · · · · · · · · · · · · · · · next to last

Beef And Broccoli Stir-fry

valid · well-founded
foreign ·unfamiliar
ought · should
kimono · · · · · · · · · · · · · · · · · Japanese robe
apparel · clothes
rife · full
tolerable · · · · · · · · · · · · · · · · · · · bearable
isolation ·alone
celestial ·heavenly
outright · · · · · · · · · · · · · · · · · · · completely

Saffron Meatballs

redoubtable · · · · · · · · · · · · · · · · formidable
fortuitous · lucky
meager · small
parsimonious · · · · · · · · · · · · · · · · · ·stingy
implement ·tool
judicious ·sensible
diaphanous · · · · · · · · · · · · · · · · · · ·delicate
preclude ·prevent
acrid · bitter
pungent · sharp

Veggie Burger

abhorrence · disgust
entrails · innards
herbivorous · · · · · · · · · · · · · · · · · · plant-eating
rue · regret
henpeck · badger
ravage · destroy
heinous · sinful
quibble · disagree
appease · allay
passive · docile

Egg Salad

decoy · snare
verdant · lush
conscientious · · · · · · · · · · · · · · · · · thorough
lexicographer · · · · · · person compiling dictionaries
rigorous · exhaustive
reluctant · · · · · · · · · · · · · · · · · · · unwilling
footnote · comment
redress · remedy
hoodwink · · · · · · · · · · · · · · · · · · · deceive
nostrum · scheme

Poached Salmon With Dill Yogurt Sauce

procedure · · · · · · · · · · · · · · · · · · · process
amenable · · · · · · · · · · · · · · · · accommodating
preparation · · · · · · · · · · · · · · · · · production
fragile · breakable
virtually · basically
unctuous · oily
subtle · delicate
conditional · · · · · · · · · · · · · · · · · dependent
restraint · control
minimize · lessen

Stuffed Peppers

presumption · · · · · · · · · · · · · · · · · · · assumption
horde· throng
bouillabaisse · · · · · · · · · · · · · · · · · · · stew
singe · · · · · · · · · · · · · · · · · · lightly burn
serpentine · · · · · · · · · · · · · · · · · ·snake-like
heifer· young cow
bosom · breast
bovine · · · · · · · · · · · · · · · · ·relating to cows/cattle
porcine · · · · · · · · · · · · · · · · · ·relating to pigs
nauseous ·sick

Étouffée

drench· ·drown
superabundance· · · · · · · · · · · · · · · · · · · excess
crustacean · · · · · · · · · · · · · · aquatic arthropod
cursory ·superficial
ocher· brownish
crystallize ·clarify
deduce· infer
insipid· boring
indelible · · · · · · · · · · · · · · · · · · permanent
massive ·huge

Polish Stuffed Cabbage

legacy ·bequest
heritage· ·birthright
pare· remove
seasonal · · · · · · · · · · · fluctuating by time of year
steep · soak
paramount· supreme
patriotism · · · · · · · · · · · · · · · · · · ·allegiance
contender · rival
phlegmatic ·placid
suffering ·troubled by

Tofu Enchiladas

theorize · hypothesize
devise · invent
trisect · divide into 3
evince · indicate
authenticity · · · · · · · · · · · · · · · · · · genuineness
critique · analyze
inchoate · undeveloped
adulterate · alter
scoundrel · rascal
exemplar · model

Ruby's Belizean Red Beans

courtesy · offered
teeming · full of
collaborate · · · · · · · · · · · · · · · · · · · cooperate
aggregate · sum
hackneyed · · · · · · · · · · · · · · · · · · · overused
distinction · · · · · · · · · · · · · · · · · · · contrast
authentic · genuine
nuance · subtlety
denote · indicate
inverse · opposite

Breakfast For Dinner (Poached Egg Florentine With Buttermilk Biscuit)

misnomer · · · · · · · · · · · · · · · · · · wrong name
comprise · · · · · · · · · · · · · · · · · · · consist of
consistency · · · · · · · · · · · · · · · · · · · density
residue · remainder
acidify · · · · · · · · · · · · · · · · · · · change into acid
qualify · be eligible
contemporary · · · · · · · · · · · · · · · · · · modern
annals · records
imbibe · drink
acknowledge · · · · · · · · · · · · · · · · · recognize

Vegetable Pot Pie

encase · enclose
reputed ·said
proletarian· · · · · · · · · · · · · · · · · · ·low-class
untoward· annoying
understate · · · · · · · · · · · · · · · · · · · underplay
reverent· ·humble
position· spot
repertory · · · · · · · · · · · · · · · · · · · collection
pioneer ·founding
indomitable· · · · · · · · · · · · · · · unconquerable

Turkey Tostada

ameliorate · · · · · · · · · · · · · · · · · · improve
wanton ·reckless
submersion · · · · · · · · · · · · · · plunged below
extravagance · · · · · · · · · · · · · · · · ·luxury
afterthought · · · · · · · · · · · · · reconsideration
arid · dry
itinerant ·moving
ambulate· walk
inland · · · · · · · · · · · · · · · · · · · landlocked
arable ·farmable

Gourmet Grilled Cheese

rightful · · · · · · · · · · · · · · · · · · ·legitimate
possession · · · · · · · · · · · · · · · · · ·ownership
designation · · · · · · · · · · · · · · · · · appellation
inception· · · · · · · · · · · · · · · · · · ·beginning
memorable · · · · · · · · · · · · · · · · ·noteworthy
homage · · · · · · · · · · · · · acknowledgment
observance· · · · · · · · · · · · · · · · celebration
modernity · · · · · · · · · · · · · · · · · present
debonair · · · · · · · · · · · · · · · · · · charming
enthused ·eager

Raspberry Lemon L-7s (Raspberry Lemon Squares)

anachronism · · · · · · · · · · · · · · · · old-fashioned
gesture · motion
demonstrate · show
coalesce · combine
colloquial · · · · · · · · · · · · · · · · · · · informal
impugn · attack
paragon · example
conformity · · · · · · · · · · · · · · · · · compliance
impetuous · · · · · · · · · · · · · · · · · · impulsive
parlance ·speech

Cinnamon Apple Strudel With Cinnamon Whipped Cream

luscious ·rich
evoke · summon
connoisseur · · · · · · · · · · · · · · · · · · ·expert
opulent · · · · · · · · · · · · · · · · · · · luxurious
regale · delight
gluttony · · · · · · · · · · · · · · · · · · ·overeating
inevitable · · · · · · · · · · · · · · · · · predictable
corpulent ·fat
abstinence · · · · · · · · · · · · · · · · · refraining
moderation · · · · · · · · · · · · · · · · ·temperance

Strawberry Rhubarb Crostata

collegian · · · · · · · · · · · · · · · ·college student
astringent · harsh
philologist · · · · · · · · · · · · · · language expert
sense · meaning
usage · treatment
imply · indicate
variant · · · · · · · · · · · · · · · · · · · alternative
dispel · eliminate
wholly ·entirely
verbatim · exactly

Nectarine Blueberry Crumble With Oatmeal Topping

impulsive · spontaneous
explicit · clear
domicile · home
hospitable · · · · · · · · · · · · · · · · · · · welcoming
propitious ·kindly
generic ·common
extrapolate· · · · · · · · · · · · · · · · · · · ·gather
vagrant · wandering
protagonist · · · · · · · · · · · · · · · · main character
peripatetic· roaming

Sweet Potato Soufflé

encourage · inspire
pernicious · harmful
banal ·commonplace
abrupt · sudden
desist· ·cease
nonexistent · · · · · · · · · · · · · · · · · · ·absent
version· ·form
potential · capacity
revival· reawakening
formidable· · · · · · · · · · · · · · · · · · impressive

Cheesecake With Nut Crust

deceive ·mislead
denominate · name
fervid· ·passionate
habitual· ·constant
confront· challenge
daring · audacious
eschew· ·escape
norm · standard
appreciate · enjoy
aberration · · · · · · · · · · · · · · · · · · · deviation

Tiramisu

brotherhood · fellowship
speculation · · · · · · · · · · · · · · · · · · conjecture
assertion · · · · · · · · · · · · · · · · · · · statement
dubious · doubtful
claimant · applicant
equivocal · · · · · · · · · · · · · · · · · · · unclear
immerse · submerge
lattice · intertwining
expressive · · · · · · · · · · · · · · · · · · passionate
eureka · bingo

Chocolate Avocado Pudding

deter · discourage
recalcitrant · · · · · · · · · · · · · · · · uncooperative
detest · loathe
comestible · · · · · · · · · · · · · · · · · · · food
commingle · · · · · · · · · · · · · · · · · · · blend
ingenuity · · · · · · · · · · · · · · · · · inventiveness
maintain · · · · · · · · · · · · · · · · · · · conserve
consummate · · · · · · · · · · · · · · · · · · complete
amalgam · mixture
gastronomic · · · · · · · · · · · · · · · · · appetizing

Zucchini Brownies

concede · surrender
preposterous · · · · · · · · · · · · · · · · · · absurd
bias · favoritism
irreverence · · · · · · · · · · · · · · · · · · disrespect
audacious · · · · · · · · · · · · · · · · · · · fearless
indicative · · · · · · · · · · · · · · · · · · suggestive
receptive · · · · · · · · · · · · · · · · · · · responsive
neutral · nonaligned
skepticism · · · · · · · · · · · · · · · · · · · doubt
advocate · · · · · · · · · · · · · · · · · · · defender

Banana Bread

primitive · crude
skeptical · doubting
primeval · ancient
infer ·conclude
torrid· hot
accouterment· · · · · · · · · · · · · · · · · · · ·accessory
conspicuous· · · · · · · · · · · · · · · · · · · ·apparent
odorous · fragrant
somniferous· · · · · · · · · · · · · · · · · · · sleeping
insomnia · · · · · · · · · · · · · · · · · · sleeplessness

Cinnamon Crème Anglaise Ice Cream

translate ·convert
piecemeal ·gradual
wee · tiny
laborious · toilsome
superb ·excellent
chagrin ·annoyance
specious· · · · · · · · · · · · · · · · · · · misleading
circumspect · · · · · · · · · · · · · · · · · cautious
ambitious · · · · · · · · · · · · · · · · · · · aspiring
precise· ·exact

Pistachio Ice Cream

drudgery ·labor
believe· ·accept
excellent · · · · · · · · · · · · · · · · · · outstanding
phenomenon · · · · · · · · · · · · · · · occurrence
bogus ·phony
nevertheless· · · · · · · · · · · · · · · · · however
fabulous· · · · · · · · · · · · · · · · · · · ·incredible
expend· spend
liquor · alcohol
specialty · · · · · · · · · · · · · · · · · · distinctive

Watermelon Granita

glacial · icy
frigid · cold
separate · divide
transmute · change
makeup · · · · · · · · · · · · · · · · · · · composition
giddy · dizzy
inebriated · drunk
energize · arouse
further · advance
nutriment · · · · · · · · · · · · · · · · nourishment

Carrot Cake

epoch · era
attenuate · reduce
concoct · create
entice · tempt
pigment · color
aesthetic · tasteful
bedaub · smear
indigestion · · · · · · · · · · · · · · · stomach pain
protuberant · · · · · · · · · · · · · · · · bulging
midriff · belly

Chocolate Cake With Mocha Buttercream

nominee · choice
out-and-out · · · · · · · · · · · · · · · · genuinely
mite · bit
plaudit · praise
nonpareil · · · · · · · · · · · · · · · · · unrivaled
ascetic · · · · · · · · · · · · · · · · · · self-denying
inveigh · utter
cite · note
sybarite · · · · · · · · · · · · · · · pleasure-seeker
check · control

Fruit Tart With Graham Cracker Crust

regimen · routine
stifle · smother
enigma · mystery
appropriate · · · · · · · · · · · · · · · · · · acceptable
modify · alter
alternative · · · · · · · · · · · · · · · · · · · option
inadvertent · · · · · · · · · · · · · · · · · accidental
facilitate · · · · · · · · · · · · · · · · · · · promote
intention · aim
disquiet · upset

Orange Cranberry Muffins

competitive · · · · · · · · · · · · · · · · · · rivalrous
thrall · bondage
vie (vying) · · · · · · · · · · · · · · · · · · compete
devout · religious
enthusiast · · · · · · · · · · · · · · · · · · fanatic
intermediate · · · · · · · · · · · · · · · · · midway
deficient · · · · · · · · · · · · · · · · · · inadequate
sardonic · · · · · · · · · · · · · · · · · · · sarcastic
abdominal · · · · · · · · · · · · · · · · · · · belly
reminiscent · · · · · · · · · · · · · · · · · remindful

Nutella (Chocolate And Hazelnut) Biscotti

manufacture · · · · · · · · · · · · · · · · · produce
vendor · seller
bountiful · · · · · · · · · · · · · · · · · · · abundant
exotic · unusual
scarce · rare
ration · allotment
plenteous · · · · · · · · · · · · · · · · · · · copious
exuberant · · · · · · · · · · · · · · · · · · enthusiastic
adore · love
proprietary · · · · · · · · · · · · · · · · · trademarked

Nougat

eccentric · bizarre
numerical · · · · · · · · · · · · · relating to numbers
recur · repeat
constellation · group
triad · · · · · · · · · · · · · · set of three (or, threesome)
tricolor · three colors
treble · three
trio · · · · · · · · · · · · · threesome (or, set of three)
transcend · surpass
tendency · inclination

White Chocolate Bark

delineate · characterize
moniker · name
ambiguous · unclear
confection · sweet
necessitate · require
render · make
indescribably · · · · · · · · · · · · · · · inexpressibly
indispensable · · · · · · · · · · · · · · · · · · necessary
repertoire · collection
revive · awaken

Baklava

adhere · stick
floral · flower
retch · vomit
repetition · · · · · · · · · · · · · · · · · · repeatedly
apiary · bee home
ironic · · · · · · · · · · · · · · · · · · · contradictory
ambivalent · · · · · · · · · · · · · · · · · · uncertain
participate · · · · · · · · · · · · · · · · · · · partake
repugnance · · · · · · · · · · · · · · · · · abhorrence
vermin · pests

Dulce De Leche Pudding

relevant ·applicable
maxim· adage
epitome· essence
interact ·mix
unison ·accord
promoter · encourager
mellifluous · flowing
redolent· fragrant
remiss · negligent
genesis· creation

Orange Tea Infused Hot Chocolate

rudimentary ·basic
quite · fully
granular· particulate
luxurious· ·extravagant
metal· · · · · · · · · · · · · · · · · · · chemical element
vestige· remnant
archaic· ancient
indigenous· native
modernize · improve
migrate ·roam

Ginger Scones

contrived ·phony
hereditary ·inherited
episode · segment
chortle· laugh
irrational · absurd
babble · chatter
humbug ·nonsense
dilute · attenuate
piquant · flavorful
incendiary · fiery

Cinnamon Rolls

witless · foolish
accurate · correct
operative ·functioning
wretched · disgusting
rendition · version
attest · affirm
aroma · smell
marvel ·amaze
benison · blessing
disparage · criticize

Shortbread Cookies Dipped In Chocolate

credible · believable
icon ·likeness
requisite ·necessary
unleavened · unraised
brittle ·fragile
antiquated · old
extension · stretching
instill · infuse
decorate · embellish
perforate · penetrate

Chocolate Chip Cookies

alias ·pseudonym
relish ·savor
fanatic · zealot
wearisome ·tired
alter ·adjust
instant · immediate
rapidly ·quickly
whereupon · · · · · · · · · · · · · · · · · · · after which
ubiquitous · · · · · · · · · · · · · · · · · · · omnipresent
pastime ·hobby

Molasses Cookies

salutary · beneficial
innocuous · harmless
spontaneously · · · · · · · · · · · · · · · automatically
undulate · flow
immense · huge
uproot · displace
wrest · pulled
wreak · cause
havoc · chaos
deluge · flood

Apple Rhubarb Sauce

botanical · plant related
enjoin · command
determination · · · · · · · · · · · · · · · · · settlement
consensus · agreement
classify · categorize
stratagem · trick
preempt · prevent
levy · collect
suffuse · cover
allure · appeal

Fruit Parfait

exclusively · solely
evolve · develop
comprehensive · · · · · · · · · · · · · · · · · inclusive
strata · layers
transparent · clear
legitimate · rightful
meander · wander
esthetic · pleasing
visualize · envision
option · choice

Poached Pears

deciduous · · · · · · · · · · · · · sheds leaves annually
poise · gracefulness
plurality · variety
forfend · prevent
arrant · downright
nefarious · foul
ailment · disease
ramose · · · · · · · · · · · · · · · having branches
paly · dull
airy · delicate

Grilled Peaches With Vanilla Mascarpone

lethargic · lazy
toilsome · · · · · · · · · · · · · · · · · · · laborious
essence · spirit
emblem · symbol
peerless · · · · · · · · · · · · · · · · · · unrivaled
finale · end
intricate · · · · · · · · · · · · · · · · · complicated
succulent · · · · · · · · · · · · · · · mouth-watering
ambrosia · · · · · · · · · · · · · · · pleasing to taste
discriminating · · · · · · · · · · · · · · · · selective

Gourmet Banana Split Sundae

fortnight · · · · · · · · · · · · · · · · · · · two weeks
intolerable · · · · · · · · · · · · · · · · insufferable
thwart · prevail
belate · delay
prompt · initiate
mollycoddle · · · · · · · · · · · · · · · · · · pamper
cognizant · aware
precipitous · · · · · · · · · · · · · · · · · · abrupt
tainted · blemished
mar · spoil

From The Back Cover

delectable · delightful
ravenous · insatiable
innovative ·original
stimulate ·activate
lachrymal ·tear
acquire ·obtain
arduous · formidable
simultaneous · · · · · · · · · · · · · · · · · · concurrent
adept· skilled
assuage ·relieve

About The Authors

Charis Freiman-Mendel has a PASSION for cooking and an AVERSION to standardized testing. "Cook Your Way Through The S.A.T." was her solution, both LITERALLY and FIGURATIVELY, for making lemonade out of lemons.

Jennie Ann Freiman is an ARDENT LOGOPHILE who is FLUMMOXED by food preparation.